Into the Silent Land

Into the Silent Land

A Guide to the Christian Practice of Contemplation

Martin Laird, O.S.A.

OXFORD
UNIVERSITY PRESS
2006

OXFORD

UNIVERSITY PRESS

Oxford University Press, Inc., publishes works that
further Oxford University's objective of excellence
in research, scholarship, and education.

Oxford   New York
Auckland   Cape Town   Dar es Salaam   Hong Kong   Karachi
Kuala Lumpur   Madrid   Melbourne   Mexico City   Nairobi
New Delhi   Shanghai   Taipei   Toronto

With offices in
Argentina   Austria   Brazil   Chile   Czech Republic   France   Greece
Guatemala   Hungary   Italy   Japan   Poland   Portugal   Singapore
South Korea   Switzerland   Thailand   Turkey   Ukraine   Vietnam

Published by Oxford University Press, Inc.
198 Madison Avenue, New York, NY 10016
www.oup.com

Library of Congress Cataloging-in-Publication Data
Laird, M. S. (Martin S.)
Into the silent land : a guide to the Christian practice
of contemplation / Martin Laird.
p. cm.
Includes bibliographical references.
ISBN-13: 978-0-19-530760-3
ISBN-10: 0-19-530760-7
1. Contemplation.
I. Title.
BV5091.C7L35   2006
248.3'4—dc22

Printed in the United States of America
on acid-free paper

For Martha Reeves,
Anglican Solitary

He who learns must suffer. And even in our sleep pain that cannot forget falls drop by drop upon the heart, and in our own despair, against our will, comes wisdom to us by the awful grace of God.

—*Aeschylus,* Agamemnon *1. 177*

By waiting and by calm you shall be saved,
in quiet and in trust your strength lies.

—*Isaiah 30:15*

Contents

Acknowledgements

Books are written largely in the wide open spaces of solitude. Like all fruitful solitude, however, it is essentially ecclesial, the gift of community. For nearly 25 years my religious Order has been a crucible of love in this regard, and I wish to thank in particular the friars and nuns of the Order of St. Augustine, especially David Brecht, O.S.A., John FitzGerald, O.S.A, Mary Grace Kuppe, O.S.A., Richard Jacobs, O.S.A., Gerald Nicholas, O.S.A., Benignus O'Rourke, O.S.A., Robert Prevost, O.S.A., Raymond Ryan, O.S.A, Theodore Tack, O.S.A., James Thompson, O.S.A., my confreres at St. Monica's Priory, Hoxton Square, London. These and many other confreres have been sources of inspiring friendship, humanity, and wisdom for many years.

Debts of gratitude are always a privilege to bear, and it would be impossible to thank enough the following who have been especially instrumental over the years. Dom Bernard (RIP) at Guadalupe Abbey, Aubrey and K. Buxton, Michael Coll, Dom Cyril at Parkminster, Christopher Daly, Kevin Hughes, Betty Maney, Pauline Matarasso, Maria Meister, Carolyn Osiek, Martha Reeves, Polly Robin, Ursula Rowlatt, Tom Smith, Werner Valentin. Villanova University has been my academic community and home for the last several years, and I remain grateful for the friendship and support of the Department of Theology and Religious Studies.

Joan Rieck is an excellent teacher and has taught me more about the true nature of silence by the lifting of a bell than by anything that could be captured in words. Tom and Monica Cornell of The Catholic Worker, Marlboro, New York, remain the kitchen table in my life and the guardians of my basement solitude.

Carmelite monasteries throughout the United Kingdom have endured with dignity and forbearance much of what is written in this book. I thank especially the Carmelite nuns at Birkenhead, Falkirk, Langham, Liverpool, Nottinghill, St. Helens, Ware, Wolverhampton, Wood Hall, York. Their courage, simplicity, honesty, God-centeredness, and kindness to this loving brother have been deeply moving and sustaining over many years.

Authors learn gratitude from editors for very good reasons. Cynthia Read and Julia TerMaat at Oxford University Press in New York have been immensely helpful and offered invaluable editorial assistance. Brendan Walsh at Darton, Longman and Todd in London sought me out on this project and has been a warm and humane source of encouragement. Elizabeth Wales was instrumental in finding this book a home.

Inspiring collections of talks by Antoinette Warner's (Gangagi) *You Are That!*, 2 vols. (Boulder, CO: Satsang Press, 1995 and 1996), gave me a new way of seeing the ancient Christian practice of awareness (especially evident in this book's epilogue).

Biblical citations throughout are from various English translations: the New Jerusalem Bible, the New American Bible, the Revised Standard Version.

Modern poetry is quoted with grateful acknowledgement to the following publishers: Bloodaxe Books for permission to quote from R. S. Thomas, *Collected Later Poems 1988– 2000* (Bloodaxe Books, 2000); the Orion Publishing Group for permission to quote from R. S. Thomas, *Collected Poems 1945–1990* (J. M. Dent, an imprint of the Orion Publsihing Group); the Goldsmith Press on behalf of Peter Kavanagh, New York, for permission to quote from Patrick Kavanagh, *Complete Poems* (The Goldsmith Press, 1988); Broughton House Books for permission to quote from Pauline Matarasso, *The Price of Admission* (Broughton House Books, Cambridge UK, 2005); A. P. Watt Ltd. on behalf of Michael B. Yeats for permission to quote from *The Poems of W. B. Yeats*, ed. J. Finneran (New York: Macmillan Publishing Company, 1983); excerpts from "The Pentecost Castle," from *New and Collected Poems 1952–1992* by Geoffrey Hill, reprinted by permission of Houghton Mifflin Company, U.S.A. and Penguin Books Ltd., UK. Every effort was made to locate the Canadian rights holder of Geoffrey Hill's "The Pentecost Castle." If the Canadian rights holder wishes to assert rights, please contact the author.

Into the Silent Land

Introduction

God Our Homeland

We must fly to our beloved homeland.
—*St. Augustine*, The City of God

We are built for contemplation. This book is about cultivating the skills necessary for this subtlest, simplest, and most searching of the spiritual arts. Communion with God in the silence of the heart is a God-given capacity, like the rhododendron's capacity to flower, the fledgling's for flight, and the child's for self-forgetful abandon and joy. If the grace of God that suffuses and simplifies the vital generosity of our lives does not consummate this capacity while we live, then the very arms of God that embrace us as we enter the transforming mystery of death will surely do so. This self-giving God, the Being of our being, the Life of our life, has joined to Himself two givens of human life: we are built to commune with God and we will all meet death.

Whether we discover the *unum necessarium*, the "one thing necessary," (Lk 10:42) during the time we are given in our lives, or whether this realization comes to us only as it came to Tolstoy's Ivan Illyich, who, finally reconciled with his sad, misshapen life so that he could move through death, exclaimed in joy at his great discovery, "And Death? Where is it?. . . There is no more death,"[1] God is our homeland. And the homing instinct of the human being is homed on God. As St. Augustine put it "we must fly to our beloved homeland. There the Father is, and there is everything."[2]

This book is guided by a practical concern: to offer guidance and encouragement for increasing our familiarity with this homeland that grounds our very selves. In his *Maxims on Love*, St. John of the Cross says, "The Father spoke one Word, which was his Son, and this Word he speaks always in eternal silence, and in silence must be heard by the soul."[3] In his Letter Seven, the same Spanish friar says, "Our greatest need is to be silent before this great God, . . . for the only language he hears is the silent language of love."[4] Silence is an urgent necessity for us; silence is necessary if we are to hear God speaking in eternal silence; our own silence is necessary if God is to hear us. Silence is necessary because, as Maggie Ross boldly puts it, "Salvation is about silence."[5]

These mutual silences are the terrain of the silent land. But unlike other landscapes there is no definitive map of this land of silence. John of the Cross, one of the greatest cartographers of the spiritual life, indicates this at the beginning of his own attempt to map this silence in *The Ascent of Mount Carmel*. Before the work begins John gives us a line drawing of what his book is to be about. He sketches Mount Carmel as a spiritual mountain, a symbol of the soul. Not too far up the base of the mountain he has written, "Here there is no longer any way because for the just man there is no law, he is a law unto himself."[6] John is not advocating any sort of lawless, just-do-as-you-like lifestyle. Rather he is indicating the intrinsically unchartable nature of silence. Pauline Matarasso captures the essence of this in her poem "Inside-out":

I look towards silence.
It is not, as I had heard, a peak
with natural footholds and the crampons left
by better climbers.

. . . .

Contrary to what they say there is no map
(they may be speaking of another place)
there is only surrender. . . . [7]

We enter the land of silence by the silence of surrender, and there is no map of the silence that is surrender. There are skills, however, by which we learn to dispose ourselves to surrender and thus to discover this uncharted land. Moreover, there is the communal support of fellow pilgrims living and dead, whose wisdom comes to us in countless writings and through innumerable acts of compassion and who teach us what it means to "walk by faith, not by sight" (2 Cor 5:7). This book is concerned with some of these skills and how the Christian tradition suggests we might cultivate them through the practice of silence.

The practice of silence, what I shall call "contemplative practice" or simply "practice" cannot be reduced to a spiritual technique. Techniques are all the rage today. They suggest a certain control that aims to determine a certain outcome. They clearly have their place. But this is not what contemplative practice does. The difference may be slight but it is an important one. A spiritual practice simply disposes us to allow something to take place. For example, a gardener does not actually grow plants. A gardener practices certain gardening skills that facilitate growth that is beyond the gardener's direct control. In a similar way, a sailor cannot produce the necessary wind that moves the boat. A sailor practices sailing skills that harness the gift of wind that brings the sailor home, but there is nothing the sailor can do to make the wind blow. And so it is with contemplative practice, not a technique, but a skill. The skill required is interior silence.

There are two contemplative practices of fundamental importance in the Christian tradition: the practice of stillness (also called meditation, still prayer, contemplative prayer, etc.) and the practice of watchfulness or awareness. These contemplative skills are not imports from other religious traditions, and the Christian contemplative tradition has a lot to say about them. While other religious traditions also have important things to say about each of these, this book will stay within the Christian tradition and address especially those who look to the Christian tradition for guidance and inspiration along the contemplative path.

The specific focus of this book will be on the practical struggles many of us face when we try to be silent—the inner chaos going on in our heads, like some wild cocktail party of which we find ourselves the embarrassed host. Often, however, we are not even aware of how utterly dominating this inner noise is until we try to enter through the doorway of silence.

The first two chapters will set the scene for these practical considerations. Chapter 1 will announce the foundational assumption that union with God is not something we are trying to acquire; God is already the ground of our being. It is a question of realizing this in our lives. Chapter 2 presents a perspective on why most of us spend most of our lives more or less ignorant of this. It is precisely this noisy, chaotic mind that keeps us ignorant of the deeper reality of God as the ground of our being. This ignorance is pervasive and renders us like the proverbial deep-sea fisherman, who spends his life fishing for minnows while standing on a whale.

The subsequent chapters address the fundamentals of contemplative practice and how these bear upon the challenges of dealing with the afflictive emotions and negotiating the perilously entertaining and subtle world of distractions. The constant point of reference will be how contemplative practice nurtures interior silence, teaches us the art of letting go, and helps us experience our struggles with greater clarity and balance.

Throughout the book I use various quotations to connect the struggles we all face to a living tradition of wisdom. By this I hope to show that the saints and sages of the Christian tradition have shared and reflected on the very yearnings and struggles we all experience. Some of the authors are well known, some less well known, some ancient, some contemporary. But apart from benefiting from their wisdom we shall see that precisely by living through our own breakdowns and breakthroughs we are initiated into the same living tradition that vitalized them. While the discovery of this silent land is deeply personal, and no one can do it for us, it is at the same time deeply communal: paradoxically no one discovers the solitude of inner silence by oneself.

God is our homeland. Dominant initiatives afoot at the present time, however, seem rather convinced that they know what God thinks, what lands God is giving to some, what lands God is taking from others. Lands of ideology, lands of aggression and violence, lands of tribal egocentricity threaten to overtake the land of hope and glory, directing the pomp and circumstance to themselves. This book, by contrast, proceeds from an ancient Christian view that the foundation of every land is silence (Ws 18:14), where God simply and perpetually gives *Himself*. This Self-gift is manifested in the creation, in the people of God and their inspired (if stumbling) pursuit of a just society, and most fully, in the Christian view of things, in Jesus Christ. This is the homeland to which every spiritual pilgrim is constantly being called, "called home," as St. Augustine says, "from the noise that is around us to the joys that are silent. Why do we rush about . . . looking for God who is here at home with us, if all we want is to be with him?"[8]

This joy that is silent is already within us. Its discovery is precious beyond compare. R. S. Thomas expresses it with deceptive understatement:

> But the silence in the mind
> is when we live best, within
> listening distance of the silence we call God . . .
> It is a presence, then,
> whose margins are our margins; that calls us out over our
> own fathoms.

This silence is all pervading, from the innermost depths of the human being, whose margins are God's margins, to the widest embrace of human compassion. "What to do," asks R. S. Thomas, "but draw a little nearer to such ubiquity by remaining still?"[9] Let us journey home, then, to the silence of our own fathoms by becoming still.

ONE

Parting the Veil:
The Illusion of
Separation from God

If the doors of perception were cleansed
Everything would appear to man as it is, infinite.

—*William Blake*

A young prisoner cuts himself with a sharp knife to dull emotional pain. "As long as I can remember," he says, "I have had this hurt inside. I can't get away from it, and sometimes I cut or burn myself so that the pain will be in a different place and on the outside." Acknowledging this to himself, he decided to approach the Prison Phoenix Trust, whose aim is to address the spiritual needs of prisoners by teaching them how to pray, how to turn their prison cells into monastic cells. After learning how to meditate and practicing it twice a day for several weeks, the young prisoner speaks movingly of what he has learnt. "I just want you to know that after only four weeks of meditating half an hour in the morning and at night, the pain is not so bad, and for the first time in my life, I can see a tiny spark of something within myself that I can like."

Another prisoner discovers he is becoming more human and realizes in the process, "All beings, no matter how reactionary, fearful, dangerous or lost, can open themselves to the sacred within and become free. I have become free even in prison. Prison is the perfect monastery."[1]

The spiritual liberation of which these prisoners speak is not something they acquired. The clear sense of their testimony is that they discovered, rather than acquired, this "sacred within." The distinction between acquisition and discovery may seem like hairsplitting, but it is important to see that what the one prisoner calls the "sacred within" did not come from some place outside him. The contemplative discipline of meditation, what I will call in this book contemplative practice, doesn't acquire anything. In that sense, and an important sense, it is not a technique but a surrendering of deeply imbedded resistances that allows the sacred within gradually to reveal itself as a simple, fundamental fact. Out of this letting go there emerges what St. Paul called our "hidden self": "may he give you the power through his Spirit for your hidden self to grow strong" (Eph 3:16). Again, contemplative practice does not produce this "hidden self" but facilitates the falling away of all that obscures it. This voice of the liberated hidden self, the "sacred within," joins the Psalmist's, "Oh, Lord, you search me and you know me. . . . It was you who created my inmost self. . . . I thank you for the wonder of my being" (Ps 138 (9):1, 13, 14).

Through their experience of interior stillness these prisoners unwittingly have joined a chorus of saints and sages who proclaim by their lives that this God we seek has already found us, already looks out of our own eyes, is already, as St. Augustine famously put it, "closer to me than I am to myself."[2] "O Beauty ever ancient, ever new," he continues, "you were within and I was outside myself."[3]

One of the more provocative books concerning life with God is known as *The Cloud of Unknowing*. It is an anonymous work from the English Middle Ages and its author, likely a Carthusian monk, is simply known as the author of *The Cloud*. In this work, as well as in a companion piece, *The Book of Privy Counselling*, the author of *The Cloud* offers much helpful advice and encouragement to anyone who feels drawn to contemplation. With startling frankness he says, "God is your being, and what you are, you are in God."[4] So as not to cause doctrinal eyebrows to spike he quickly qualifies his statement, "But you are not God's being."[5]

Not only has this God we desire already found us, thus causing our desire, but God has never *not* found us. "It was you who created my inmost self and put me together in my mother's womb. You know me through and through, from having watched my bones take shape when I was being formed in secret" (Ps 139:13–15). "Before I formed you in the womb, I knew you" (Jer 1:5). As Creator, God is the ground of who we are.

"God is your being." The author of *The Cloud* is not an isolated voice in this matter. The great Carmelite doctor of the Church, St. John of the Cross, says, "The soul's center is God."[6] God is the ground of the human being. Various Christian traditions may argue over orthodox or heterodox ways of understanding this, but there is clear and authoritative testimony based on living the Christian mysteries that if we are going to speak of what a human being is, we have not said enough until we speak of God. If we are to discover for ourselves who we truly are—that inmost self that is known before it is formed, ever hidden with Christ in God (Ps 139:13; Jer 1:5; Col 3:3)—the discovery is going to be a manifestation of the ineffable mystery of God, though we may feel more and more inclined to say less and less about God. As St. Diadochos of Photiki observed, there are some who are adept in the spiritual life and "consciously illuminated by spiritual knowledge, yet do not speak about God."[7]

Union with God is not something that needs to be acquired but realized. The reality, which the term "union" points to (along with a host of other metaphors), is already the case. The unfolding in our lives of this fundamental union is what St. John of the Cross called "the union of likeness."[8] It is our journey from image to likeness (Gen 1:26).

Acquisition and its strategies obviously have a role in life. It is important to pursue and acquire good nutrition, reasonable health, a just society, basic self-respect, the material means by which to live, and a host of other things. However, they don't have a real role in the deeper dynamics of life. For example, they play no role in helping us to die or to become aware of God. Dying is all about letting go and letting be, as is the awareness of God.

People who have traveled far along the contemplative path are often aware that the sense of separation from God is itself pasted up out of a mass of thoughts and feelings. When the mind comes into its own stillness and enters the silent land, the sense of separation goes. Union is seen to be the fundamental reality and separateness a highly filtered mental perception. It has nothing whatever to do with the loss of one's ontological status as a creature of God, nothing to do with becoming an amorphous blob. Quite the opposite, it is the realization this side of death of the fundamental mystery of our existence as the creation of a loving God. "Of you my heart has spoken, 'seek His face'" (Ps 27:8). "For God alone my soul in silence waits" (Ps 62:1,6). "God is your being, and what you are you are in God, but you are not God's being."[9] "You have made us for yourself, O Lord, and our heart is restless until it rests in you."[10]

Once this depth dimension of life emerges, New Testament resonances, especially with John and Paul, reach the whole world (Ps 19:4). John's Gospel is well known for its concern for this divine indwelling. "On that day you will know that I am in my Father and you are in me and I in you" (Jn 14:20). "May they all be one, just as, Father, you are in me and I am in you, so that they also may be in us." (Jn 17:21).

Paul, the author of the oldest New Testament writings we have, is an important witness to this. In the Letter to the Galatians he writes, "I have been Crucified with Christ and yet I am alive; yet it is no longer I, but Christ living in me" (Gal 2:19). Paul looks within and sees not Paul but Christ. Are Paul and Christ two separate things? They are two separate things from the perspective of creation, yes, but from the perspective of the transformation of awareness, no. When Paul looks within and sees Christ, I do not suggest he sees Christ as an object of awareness. Paul speaks of something more direct and immediate, which pertains to the ground of awareness and not to the objects of awareness. The awareness itself is somehow about the presence of Christ in Paul. "I live now, not I, but Christ lives in me." Paul has not used the word "union," but he's getting at the same reality that the language of union attempts to express. Obviously, a CCTV camera watching Paul say all this is going to show the same old Paul. This has to do with the ground of awareness, not what he's *aware of*, but the ground of the *aware-ing* itself. Only when the mind is held by silence does this open field of awareness emerge as the unifying ground of all unities and communities, the ground of all that is, all life, all intelligence.

Whatever this "Christ-living-in-me" is, and it is most assuredly not a particular *thing*, it holds true for each of us. My

Christ-self is your Christ-self, our enemy's Christ-self (2 Cor 10:7). A helpful image to express this sort of thing is a wheel with spokes centered on a single hub. The hub of the wheel is God; we the spokes. Out on the rim of the wheel the spokes are furthest from one another, but at the center, the hub, the spokes are most united to each other. They are a single meeting in the one hub. The image was used in the early church to say something important about that level of life at which we are one with each other and one with God. The more we journey towards the Center the closer we are both to God and to each other. The problem of feeling isolated from both God and others is overcome in the experience of the Center. This journey into God and the profound meeting of others in the inner ground of silence is a single movement. Exterior isolation is overcome in interior communion.

Those who sound alarms regarding the realization of the contemplative path as being anticommunity reveal a shocking ignorance of this simple fact: the personal journey into God is simultaneously ecclesial and all-embracing. This in part is why people who have gone fairly deeply into the contemplative path, become open and vital people (however differently they may live this out). In this depthless depth we are caught up in a unity that grounds, affirms, and embraces all diversity. Communion with God and communion with others are realizations of the same Center. And this Center, according to the ancient definition, is everywhere. "God is that reality whose centre is everywhere and whose circumference is nowhere."[11]

For Paul it is precisely baptism that accomplishes this union. He writes in the Letter to the Galatians: "As many of you as were baptized into Christ have clothed yourselves with Christ.

There is no longer Jew or Greek, there is no longer slave or free, there is no longer male and female; for all of you are one in Christ Jesus" (Gal 3:27–28). The indwelling presence of Christ is not only the core of human identity, but also something (a something that's not a thing) that resolves dualities, which, at more superficial levels of awareness, appear to be opposites.

Paul describes in the First Letter to the Colossians what baptism accomplishes. "Because you have died, the life you now have is hidden with Christ in God. . . . Christ is your life . . . you too will be revealed in all your glory with Christ" (Col 3:1–4). When Paul describes our life as being hidden with Christ in God, he is not using the word "life" in the sense that one's career is one's life, "being a doctor is my life," "my children are my life." He's talking about something much deeper: what makes you exist rather than not exist. Paul and the author of *The Cloud* are very much on the same wavelength. The latter says, "God is your being," and Paul to the people of Athens says that in God "we live and move and have our being" (Acts 17:28).[12] When Paul says our life is something that is "hidden with Christ in God," I think we should hear him saying something about our deepest self.

There is a lot of talk in contemporary theology and philosophy about what a "self" is. One wonders how much of it Paul would have been able to follow, or care about for that matter. But he does have something evocative to contribute: your life, your "self," who you truly are, is something that is "hidden with Christ in God." Whatever there is about human identity that can be objectively known, measured, predicted, observed, whether by the Myers-Briggs, the Enneagram, the tax man, or the omniscient squint of your most insightful aunt, there is a foundational core of what we might as well call identity that remains hidden from scrutiny's grip and somehow utterly caught up in God, "in whom we live and move and have our being," in whom our very self is immersed.

Precisely because our deepest identity, grounding the personality, is hidden with Christ in God and beyond the grasp of comprehension, the experience of this ground-identity that is one with God will register in our perception, if indeed it does register, as an experience of no particular thing, a great, flowing abyss, a depthless depth. To those who know only the discursive mind, this may seem a death-dealing terror or spinning vertigo. But for those whose thinking mind has expanded into heart-mind, it is an encounter brimming over with the flow of vast, open emptiness that is the ground of all. This "no thing," this "emptiness" is not an absence but a superabundance. It is the fringe of love's cloak (Matt 9:20). "Where can I run from your love; where can I flee from your presence. If I climb to the heavens you are there, there too if I lie in Sheol" (Ps 138:7–8).

One need not have journeyed too far into this silent land to realize that the so-called psychological self, our personality (not what Paul is talking about as hidden with Christ in God) is a cognitive construct pasted up out of thoughts and feelings. A rather elaborate job has been done of it, and it is singularly useful. But our deepest identity, in which thoughts and feelings appear like patterns of weather on Mount Zion (Ps 125), remains forever immersed in the silence of God. The baptism of which Paul speaks (Col 3:1–4; Gal 3:27–28) heralds a fundamental truth about our lives: the God we seek has from all eternity sought and found us (Jer 1:5) and is shining out our eyes.

For Christians the Eucharist likewise proclaims this foundational union with God. Preaching on the Eucharist in his Hom-

ily on the Feast of Pentecost, Augustine says to his congrega-
tion, "You are the mystery that is placed upon the Lord's table.
You receive the mystery that is yourself. To that which you are,
you will respond, 'Amen.'"[13] Much later John Ruysbroeck speaks
of our union with God through the Eucharist in an almost
overwhelming manner. "He enters the very marrow of our
bones. . . . He consumes us without ever statisfying this illim-
itable hunger and immeasurable thirst. . . . He swoops upon
us like a bird of prey to consume our whole life, that he may
change it into His."[14]

Baptism and Eucharist are the great sacraments of God's
self-giving. They create, cultivate, and sustain the foundational
unity between God and humanity that is manifested in Christ.
These are the sacraments of our deepest identity, hidden in
the self-emptying of God in Christ.

Union with God is not something we acquire by a technique but the grounding truth of our lives that engenders the
very search for God. Because God is the ground of our being,
the relationship between creature and Creator is such that, by
sheer grace, separation is not possible. God does not know
how to be absent. The fact that most of us experience throughout most of our lives a sense of absence or distance from God
is the great illusion that we are caught up in; it is the human
condition. The sense of separation from God is real, but the
meeting of stillness reveals that this perceived separation does
not have the last word. This illusion of separation is generated by the mind and is sustained by the riveting of our attention to the interior soap opera, the constant chatter of the
cocktail party going on in our heads. For most of us this is
what normal is, and we are good at coming up with ways of
coping with this perceived separation (our consumer-driven

entertainment culture takes care of much of it). But some of us are not so good at coping, and so we drink ourselves into oblivion or cut or burn ourselves "so that the pain will be in a different place and on the outside."[15]

The grace of salvation, the grace of Christian wholeness that flowers in silence, dispels this illusion of separation. For when the mind is brought to stillness, and all our strategies of acquisition have dropped, a deeper truth presents itself: we are and have always been one with God and we are all one in God (Jn 17:21). The marvelous world of thoughts, sensation, emotions, and inspiration, the spectacular world of creation around us, are all patterns of stunning weather on the holy mountain of God. But we are not the weather. We are the mountain. Weather is happening—delightful sunshine, dull sky, or destructive storm—this is undeniable. But if we think we are the weather happening on Mount Zion (and most of us do precisely this with our attention riveted to the video), then the fundamental truth of our union with God remains obscured and our sense of painful alienation heightened. When the mind is brought to stillness we see that we are the mountain and not the changing patterns of weather appearing on the mountain. We are the awareness in which thoughts and feelings (what we take to be ourselves) appear like so much weather on Mount Zion.

For a lifetime we have taken this weather—our thoughts and feelings—to be ourselves, taken ourselves to be this video to which the attention is riveted. Stillness reveals that we are the silent, vast awareness in which the video is playing. To glimpse this fundamental truth is to be liberated, to be set free from the fowler's snare (Ps 123:7). "Who ever trusts in the Lord is like Mount Zion: Unshakeable, it stands forever"

(Ps 125:1). "Mount Zion, true pole of the earth, the great King's city" (Ps 48:2).

Some who are tediously metaphysical might worry that all this talk of union with God blurs the distinction between Creator and creation. Far from blurring this distinction it sets it in sharper focus. John's Gospel says we are the branches and Christ is the vine. (Jn 15:5). The branches are not separate from the vine but one with it. If the branch is cut off, you won't have a branch, for it soon shrivels away. A branch is a branch insofar as it is one with the vine. From the branch's perspective it is all vine. Speaking of this transformation of consciousness that marks the moving into awareness of our grounding union with God, Meister Eckhart says, "All things become pure God to you, for in all things you see nothing but God."[16] John of the Cross speaks along similar lines. "It seems to [the soul] that the entire universe is a sea of love in which it is engulfed, for, conscious of the living point or center of love within itself, it is unable to catch sight of the boundaries of this love."[17] When life is lived from "the center," as John of the Cross terms it, all of life seems shot through with God.

We might liken the depths of the human to the sponge in the ocean. The sponge looks without and sees ocean; it looks within and sees ocean. The sponge is immersed in what at the same time flows through it. The sponge would not be a sponge were this not the case. Some call this differentiating union: the more we realize we are one with God the more we become ourselves, just as we are, just as we were created to be. The Creator is outpouring love, the creation, the love outpoured.

Union with God respects all distinctions between creation and Creator and is characterized by awareness of the presence and the transparency of perceived boundaries. When our awareness loosens its arthritic grip to reveal a palm open and soft, awareness is silent and vast in the depths of the present moment. As Meister Eckhart put it, "The eye with which I see God is exactly the same eye with which God sees me. My eye and God's eye are one eye, one seeing, one knowledge and one love."[18] John of the Cross expresses the same mystery. "The soul that is united and transformed in God breathes God in God with the same divine breathing with which God, while in her, breathes her in himself."[19] This is the revelation of stillness.

When our life in God washes onto the shores of perception we see no image or shape, no holy pictures or statues, nothing for thinking mind's comprehending grip. We know undeniably, like the back of our hand, the silent resounding of a great and flowing vastness that is the core of all. Words cannot express it (2 Cor 12:4). No tongue has sullied it. Such is the impenetrable silence in which we are immersed. Yet this silence cleanses the mind and unbinds the tongue. "I will sing, I will sing your praise. Awake my soul. Awake lyre and harp. I will awake the dawn" (Ps 56:7–8).

The Wild Hawk of the Mind

Hands do what you're bid:
Bring the balloon of the mind
That bellies and drags in the wind
Into its narrow shed.

—*W. B. Yeats*

Too fidgety the mind's compass.

—*R. S. Thomas*

When pummeled by too many thoughts a long walk would cure me of the punch-drunk feeling of lifelessness. The normal route led along open fields, and not infrequently I would see a man walking his four Kerry blue terriers. These were amazing dogs. Bounding energy, elastic grace, and electric speed, they coursed and leapt through open fields. It was invigorating just to watch these muscular stretches of freedom race along. Three of the four dogs did this, I should say. The fourth stayed behind and, off to the side of its owner, ran in tight circles. I could never understand why it did this; it had all the room in the world to leap and bound. One day I was bold enough to ask the owner, "Why does your dog do that? Why does it run in little circles instead of running with the others?" He explained that before he acquired the dog, it had lived practically all its life in a cage and could only exercise by running in circles. For this dog, to run meant to run in tight circles. So instead of bounding through the open fields that surrounded it, it ran in circles.

This event has always stayed with me as a powerful metaphor of the human condition. For indeed we are free, as the Psalmist insists, "My heart like a bird has escaped from the snare of the fowler" (Ps 123:7). But the memory of the cage remains. And so we run in tight, little circles, even while immersed in open fields of grace and freedom.

The mind's obsessive running in tight circles generates and sustains the anguish that forms the mental cage in which we live much of our lives—or what we take to be our lives. This cage can be comfortable enough; that dog wagged its tail all day long. But the long-term effects on humans can still be pretty damaging. It makes us believe we are separate from God. God then becomes an object somewhere over there in the distance and as much in need of appeasement as praise.[1] This tyrant-god is generated by the illusion of separateness and requires us to live in a mental prison (however lavishly furnished). It makes us believe that we are alone, shameful, stupid, afraid, unloveable. We believe this lie, and our life becomes a cocktail party of posturing masquerade in order to hide the anxiety and ignorance of who we truly are.

THE INTERIOR VIDEO

The woman could blow like silk across the stage or drive like a storm through the corps de ballet. To watch this world-class ballerina was to behold light and grace in human form. But if you would ask her about her own experience as source of beauty and inspiration you would see only a vacant stare of shocked disbelief. She would speak instead of an obsessive and torturously perfectionist mind that left her grinding her teeth. She described her inner state as a series of internal videos that constantly played and that she constantly watched. Her attention was routinely stolen by them.

What were these videos that played in her head? Usually something about how she wasn't quite up to standard—not just regarding ballet but *any* aspect of her life. This accompanied another series of videos concerning her intense anger. The anger registered in her body as a clenched jaw and a physique completely free of any suggestion of fat. Deeper than the anger, though, was the fear: fear of what the critics might say of her dancing, fear that her husband might wake up one day and decide to leave her, fear of being alone.

There were a lot of videos about pain. The most debilitating concerned some very old pain from childhood. One day her mother walked into her bedroom as she sat looking at herself in the mirror. The mother said to her, "I hope you don't think you're beautiful." She was indeed beautiful. In every season of life—as a young girl, an adolescent, a young adult, a mature woman—she was beautiful. But this beauty became a gag knotted behind her: for she believed she was ugly. When as a teenager she won a highly prized scholarship to study ballet, her mother said, "Why would they give you that? Everybody knows you've got two left feet." And so, although she has danced to great acclaim all over the world, she believes she's a klutz with two left feet. All of this plays in her head. Even if she isn't watching the video and pressing rewind to watch it again, and then again, and yet again, the video still plays in the background, like that dirge music in malls and lifts. This video was the cage that kept her running in tight circles.

She did find solace. She took long walks out on the York-shire moors. If she walked long enough, her roiling mind would begin to settle. The expanse of heather was scented balm that soothed the throbbing anger, fear, and pain. She described how on one occasion her anxiety began to drop like layers of scarves. Suddenly she was aware of being immersed in a sacred presence that upheld her and everything.

While this experience out on the moors happened only once, it proved a real turning point in her life and drew her into the way of prayer. She knew from her own experience that there was something in her that was deeper than her pain and anxiety and that when the chaos of the mind was quieted, the sense of anguish gave way to a sense of divine presence. R. S. Thomas recounts this sentiment movingly in his poem, "The Moor."[2]

> It was like church to me.
> I entered it on soft foot,
> Breath held like a cap in the hand.
> It was quiet.
> What God was there made himself felt,
> Not listened to, in clean colours
> That brought a moistening of the eye,
> In movement of the wind over grass.
>
> There were no prayers said. But stillness
> Of the heart's passions—that was praise
> Enough; and the mind's cession
> Of its kingdom. I walked on,
> Simple and poor, while the air crumbled
> And broke on me generously as bread.

What both the ballet dancer and R. S. Thomas seem to realize is that our own awareness, our own interiority, runs deeper than we realize. If we turn within and see only noise, chaos, thinking, anxiety—what R. S. Thomas calls "the mind's kingdom," then we have not seen deeply enough into the vast and expansive moors of human awareness. When the wandering, roving mind grows still, when fragmented craving grows still, when the "heart's passions" are rapt in stillness, then is "the mind's cession of its kingdom," a great letting go as a deeper dimension of the human person is revealed. From this depth God is seen to be the ground of both peace and chaos, one with ourselves and one with all the world, the ground "in whom we live and move and have our being" (Acts 17:28). This depth of silence is more than the mere absence of sound and is the key. As R. S. Thomas puts it, "the silence holds with its gloved hand the wild hawk of the mind."[3]

Followers of the Christian path have been singing this song of silence for centuries. In his *Confessions* St. Augustine goes so far as to say that the discovery of the various levels of silence is what it means to "Enter into the joy of your Lord" (Mt 25: 21).[4] St. John Climacus says, "The friend of silence comes close to God."[5] Meister Eckhart says, "The noblest attainment in this life is to be silent and let God work and speak within."[6] John of the Cross says, "The Father spoke one Word, which was His Son, and this Word He always speaks in eternal silence, and in silence must It be heard by the soul."[7] In the *Cherubinic Wanderer* Angelus Silesius says, "God far exceeds all words that we can here express. In silence he is heard, in silence worshipped best."[8]

What is this silence? It is certainly more than the mere absence of physical sound. More important to realize, however, is that this ineffable reality that the word "silence" points to is not something that we need to acquire, like a piece of software we can install in the computer of our spiritual lives. It is pointing to something that is already within us, grounding all mental processes, whether precise, disciplined thinking or chaotic mental obsession.

LEARNED IGNORANCE AND THE GROUND OF SILENCE

Alice and George were getting ready to celebrate their sixtieth wedding anniversary. They wanted to show me photos of grandchildren born since the celebration of their fiftieth anniversary. Alice called for George to produce the photos, and he began to fumble through various pockets, saying at each, "Right. Here they are," only to produce a hanky, a pipe, spectacles missing since last Christmas, everything but the photos in question. George suddenly remarked, "Oh dear, I changed jackets just before we left. They must be at home in the other jacket." There were some disapproving looks and muttering coming from the direction of Alice. He excused himself to go to the men's room. When he was just out of earshot (about ten feet), Alice sighed in exasperation and said, "I know him like the back of my hand but I'll never understand him." The statement was followed by engaged silence, and the moment was thick with meaning. I think anyone would understand the point she is making. In fact she is drawing an important distinction between different ways of knowing.

She is aware that there is her thinking mind, or to use a more technical term, her discursive reason—that aspect of consciousness we all use to master facts and understand things like bank balances, shopping lists, mathematics, anniversary celebrations, the behavior of spouses. But she is also aware that this level of her mind cannot grasp, cannot comprehend, all there is to her husband. And yet there is every sense of deep familiarity and real communion with this level of person where the comprehension of discursive reason does not reach. "I know him like the back of my hand but I will never understand him." Her unknowing goes deeper than her knowing, and in this depth is communion. And so it is with our life in God.

Our unknowing goes deeper into God than our knowing goes. Seasoned familiarity with God, yet complete incomprehension of God moved Augustine to call this deeper dimension of awareness "learned ignorance."[9]

Our information culture, however, exalts discursive, logical reason as the most noteworthy accomplishment of the mind. Dickens delighted in poking fun at this with wicked sarcasm in the opening lines of *Hard Times*. "Now what we want is, Facts. Teach these boys and girls nothing but Facts. Facts alone are wanted in life. Plant nothing else, rout out everything else. . . . In this life we want nothing but Facts, sir; nothing but Facts!"[10] The thinking mind is indeed a marvel, but simple life experience, such as that of Alice, suggests that thinking is not the only aspect of awareness. There are deeper dimensions that must be awakened and engaged; in fact the contemplative tradition has claimed this for centuries. It is crucial to see this in order to understand its fundamental orientation to prayer.

St. Augustine speaks of a higher part of the mind reserved for the contemplation of God and a lower part of the mind that reasons.[11] Evagrius of Pontus, a fourth-century monk, is one of a host of contemplative writers to make an important distinction between the calculating, reasoning mind that makes use of concepts in a process we call ratiocination or discursive thought, and that dimension of mind that comes to knowledge directly, without the mediation of concepts. This later he called *nous*, an intuitive spiritual intelligence. And so when he defines prayer as "communion of the mind with God,"[12] he means a dimension of our consciousness that runs deeper than the discursive process of ratiocination. Alice can know George in a deep way and still not know everything *about* George (perhaps even next to nothing). "I know him like the back of my hand but I'll never understand him." Likewise we can speak of knowing God without thinking that our thoughts and words actually grasp God. These are different forms of knowing, different forms of awareness. St. Thomas Aquinas takes up this same distinction and can be said to speak for virtually the entire tradition when he calls this aspect of mind that thinks and calculates "lower reason" (*ratio inferior*) and that aspect of the mind that communes directly with God in contemplation "higher reason" (*ratio superior*).[13] Standing on the shoulders of everyone, Dante states it most succinctly in *The Divine Comedy*, "Reason, even when supported by senses, has short wings."[14]

Closer perhaps to our own sensibilities is someone like St. Diadochos who distinguishes between the mind and the heart. He uses the term "heart" to refer to this nonconceptual form of knowing, what Augustine and Aquinas will later call "higher reason." For Diadochos, and indeed for many others after him, the heart was not the seat of emotions (emotions would be located at roughly the same level as thoughts) but the deep center of the person. The heart communes with God in a silent and direct way that the conceptual level of our mind does not.

Writing much later but from this same spiritual tradition is a remarkably gentle and insightful monk, Theophan, who says,

"You must descend from your head to your heart. At present your thoughts of God are in your head. And God Himself is, as it were, outside you, and so your prayer and other spiritual exercises remain exterior. Whilst you are still in your head, thoughts will not easily be subdued but will always be whirling about, like snow in winter or clouds of mosquitoes in the summer."[15]

This thinking mind that "whirls about" is constantly concerned with thoughts, concepts, and images, and we obviously need this dimension of mind to meet the demands of the day, to think, to reflect on and enjoy life. But the thinking mind has a professional hazard. If it is not engaged in its primary task of reason, given half a chance it fizzes and boils with obsessive thoughts and feelings. There are, however, deeper demands, deeper encounters of life, love, and God, and there is far more to being alive than riding breathlessly around in the emotional roller coaster of obsessive thinking.

This requires, however, the awakening and cultivation of the "heart-mind," to stretch Theophan's term a bit. In fact, precisely because we *think* our lives, *think* our spirituality, *think* about God, we end up perceiving God as some "thing" over there, some cause among many other causes of things. Thoughts about God make God appear, as Theophan says, "outside you." Theophan is but one of a host of saints and sages who attest that thinking about God is a problem if you want to commune with God. In fact, because our attention is so completely riveted to what's playing on the big screen of our thinking mind, we can live completely unaware of the deeper ground of the heart that already communes with God, that knows only communion, as branches know deeply the vine (Jn 15:5).

Therefore, when Theophan speaks of descending from "your head into your heart," he does not mean what modern pop psychology means when it says we must get out of our heads and feel our feelings. He means shift your attention from the screen of thinking mind on which both thoughts and feelings incessantly appear, as they are meant to, to the ground of the heart, this immense valley of awareness itself in which thoughts and feelings appear. Theophan says, "Images, however sacred they may be, retain the attention outside, whereas at the time of prayer the attention must be within—in the heart. The concentration of attention in the heart—this is the starting point of prayer."[16] This shifting of the attention from the objects of awareness to the silent vastness of the heart that is awareness itself will bring the thinking mind to silence, and the silence "holds with its gloved hand the wild hawk of the mind."[17]

"What riches does every person have inside without needing to dig!"[18] God is the ground of our being, and union with God is foundational to our humanity. "Before I formed you in the womb, I knew you" (Jer 1:5). And God still knows us in this way. As the Psalmist sings, "You know me through and through" (Ps 139:14).

Yet we don't normally have much awareness of this most fundamental reality. We go off in search of what has from all eternity sought and found us. This setting off in the wrong direction sustains a profound moral and intellectual ignorance, whose fruit is a sense of alienation from God, from self, from others. God is the ground of our innermost being, yet we skim along on the surface of life. The result is that our lives are rather like that of the deep-sea fisherman who was fishing for minnows while standing on a whale. "You were within me and I was outside myself," as Augustine famously put it.[19]

This sense of separation from God and from one another, this profound ignorance of our innermost depths, presents a singularly convincing case. This is the human condition, and we have all eaten of this fruit. But this is a lie. It is a lie spun largely out of inner noise and mental clutter. It is the inner video that plays again and again and again and steals our attention so that we overlook the simplest of truths: we are already one with God. The Christian contemplative tradition addresses this very problem by exposing the lie and introducing stillness to the mental chatter.

In the three chapters that follow I would like to discuss some of the basics of contemplative practice: how the body's own physical stillness in prayer contributes immensely to the cultivation of interior stillness; how the use of a prayer word addresses the problem of the wandering mind; how to meet the many distractions that will try, sift, and train anyone who would enter this silent land of our own being.

THREE

The Body's Call to Prayer

Let us sit still.

—Evagrius

Mr. Duffy lived at a little distance from his body.

—James Joyce

The character of Dinah in George Eliot's *Adam Bede* is surely among the most brilliant portrayals of Christian ministry-in-action that one will ever read. Among the more moving manifestations of this Methodist preacher's character is Eliot's description of Dinah sitting in prayer. Preparing to leave the community to whom she has ministered for some time, Dinah sits by her bedroom window thinking of these beloved people and their struggles. "And the pressure of this thought soon became too strong for her to enjoy the unresponding stillness of the moonlit fields. She closed her eyes, that she might feel more intensely the presence of a Love and Sympathy deeper and more tender than was breathed from the earth and sky. That was Dinah's mode of praying in solitude. Simply to close her eyes, and to feel herself enclosed by the Divine Presence; then gradually her fears, yearning anxieties for others, melted away like ice-crystals in a warm ocean."[1]

This glimpse into Dinah's personal prayer reveals important elements of the practice of contemplation. Dinah is aware of the prayerful quality of nature, "the stillness of the moonlit fields." She is aware of the burden of her thoughts: her anxieties concerning the people she has so lovingly served. When she focuses her attention within, she becomes aware of the Divine Presence in which her worries vanish. I shall have more to say in subsequent chapters concerning stillness and the struggle with thoughts but for the moment notice her "mode of praying in solitude": Dinah sits physically still and in silence. These are some of the essentials of contemplative practice that give birth to contemplation. This chapter will describe three components of contemplative practice: posture, the use of a prayer word, and the breath.

POSTURE

In C. S. Lewis's *The Screwtape Letters*, a young demon-in-training, Wormwood, is instructed by his experienced uncle, Screwtape, on the importance of keeping humans ignorant of the role of the body in prayer. "My Dear Wormwood, . . . At the very least, they [humans] can be persuaded that the bodily position makes no difference to their prayers; for they constantly forget, what you must always remember, that they are animals and that whatever their bodies do affects their souls."[2] The body has two important contributions to contemplative practice: the body's physical stillness and the breath itself. The stillness of the body facilitates the stilling of the discursive mind. Most of us spend most of our time with our attention riveted to the video going on in our heads, leaving us in a state rather like that of Mr. Duffy in James Joyce's "The Painful Case": "He lived at a little distance from his body."[3] Physical stillness returns us to living life in our bodies, as St. John Climacus put it, enclosing what is bodiless within the body.[4]

Though not especially well developed, there is an ancient Christian awareness that physical stillness facilitates interior stillness. Evagrius says, "Let us sit still and keep our attention fixed within ourselves, so that we advance in holiness and resist vice more strongly."[5] Evagrius is aware that the simple act of sitting still is an effective aid in the practice of vigilance and in keeping the attention from being stolen by thoughts. St. Gregory of Sinai and St. Gregory of Palamas both thought that sitting still and close to the floor could be of great assistance. Gregory of Sinai recommended sitting on a small stool, low to the ground. Today we call this a prayer bench.

Many of these old monks spoke of a rather odd posture that involved sitting on a low stool and bending the head down towards the navel (this is the likely origin of the term, "navel gazers"). But today we see things differently. While it is important to remember that we can pray in any position, certain positions are more suited to still prayer, and many Christian contemplatives have come to see the benefits of an erect and stable sitting posture. Largely through a sustained dialogue with Hindu and Buddhist monasticism begun in earnest by Pope Paul VI, many Christian contemplatives have seen the benefits of the classic lotus, half lotus, etc. All things being equal, they are well worth learning and can be found in any good book on yoga or Zen. Most Western Christian contemplatives, however, sit on a chair or a prayer bench. In any case there is nothing magical or esoteric about learning proper posture.

If you sit in a chair, better to use a simple flat-seated desk or kitchen chair rather than an arm chair more suited to knitting, reading, or nodding off. The idea is that the knees and the buttocks form a tripod that serves as a solid support for the body. Because most of us are so accustomed to slouching, this takes some attention.

Sit on the front portion of the seat. Don't lean back. Instead, keep the back straight; shoulders back but not rigid. Depending on your height, a lot of desk chairs leave your knees about even with your hips. If possible place a cushion under you to elevate the buttocks so that the hips are slightly above the knees. The elevation of the hips above the knees opens up the abdomen for proper breathing. Feet are flat on the floor. There should be a sense of being solid, a sense of not having to expend energy to sit up. Many people never know what to do with their hands. Just lay them palms down on the knees or gently cupped in the lap. Some find they struggle less with distractions if they keep their eyes closed. Others find that closed eyes increase distractions and so keep them slightly open but without focusing on any particular object. With time you discover which is better for you.

THE USE OF A PRAYER WORD

Because the following chapter is devoted entirely to the use of a prayer word, here a brief orientation to the prayer word will suffice. It takes less than a minute of attempting to practice inner stillness to realize that however fidgety the body may be the real obstacle to inner silence is the mind. Even when it is not performing its noble function of discursive reason and reflection, the mind is constantly on the move. As R. S. Thomas expressed it, "too fidgety the mind's compass."[6]

At times the mind flits like a finch from branch to branch and at other times it is like the three-headed dog, Cerberus, unable to decide from which bowl which of its heads should feed at any given moment. Then again, and more often than we may like to admit, the mind is as uninspired and limp as a mildewed dish cloth. The mind has countless faces. For centuries the advice of the contemplative tradition has been: well, then, give the mind something to do. If it can't be still, give it a short phrase or a word to repeat silently. And so when we sit, we give our attention wholly to the gentle repetition of the prayer word. We will find that our attention is forever being stolen. As soon as we become aware that our attention has been stolen by some thought, we gently bring ourselves back to the prayer word.

Where do we get this prayer word? For Christians we normally take it from scripture or scripturally based words. We find a word or short phrase we feel drawn to, such as "Father," "God," "Abba," "Jesus Mercy," "Holy Spirit, pray in me," etc. Perhaps the most well known prayer word is in fact a sentence, taken here and there from scripture, known as the Jesus Prayer. It has various forms, but the most well known is perhaps, "Jesus Christ, Son of God, have mercy on me." There is a slightly longer version: "Lord Jesus Christ, Son of the living God, have mercy on me, a sinner." Many simply use the essential component of the Jesus Prayer, "Jesus." Whatever prayer word we take up, we give our attention wholly to it during the time we set aside for prayer, as well as whenever we don't need to be using the mind's reasoning faculty. We don't reflect upon the meaning of the prayer word. We simply repeat it.

At the beginning, this may seem a somewhat artificial and laborious practice, but with time it becomes second nature to us. We find a home and refuge in it. Throughout all of this, the basic practice remains the same: whenever we find that our attention has been stolen by a thought—and they are as innumerable as they are subtle—we gently bring our attention back to the silent repetition of the prayer word. Our contemplative practice will be considerably deepened if we unite the practice of the prayer word with the breath.

"BREATH HELD LIKE A CAP IN THE HAND": THE BREATH IN CHRISTIAN TRADITION

Christians are sometimes thrown by the suggestion that the breath can make a significant contribution to interior silencing. "This must be a Hindu or Buddhist concern that is creeping in." While it is indeed true that working with the breath is a component of some Hindu and Buddhist contemplative disciplines, there is also a Christian tradition that advocates simple attention to the breath as an aid to deepening stillness. Before we consider, however, the Christian teaching on the role of breath in prayer and suggest how it can be integrated into contemplative practice, it should be said that we are talking about something that is quite natural.

In any activity that requires concentrated effort, the breath quite naturally plays a role. If you have ever tried to thread a needle, repair a watch or necklace, rub a speck of bird-dropping off the car, remove the swallowed hook from the fish you caught, you might have observed that without even thinking about it the breath quietens and deepens. Singers, swimmers, people who struggle with panic attacks, and a host of others learn the importance of proper breathing in order to help negotiate the respective tasks at hand. The fact, then, that the art of contemplative practice can be facilitated by the breath should come as no surprise nor suggest anything esoteric.

From early on Christians have seen breath as a potent metaphor of divine presence and somehow a fertile divine-human delta. "Then the Lord God formed man from the dust of the ground, and breathed into his nostrils the breath of life; and the man became a living being" (Gen 2:7). The inflow of God's breath quickened life in the human, and we shall see later that some Christian contemplatives have seen that attention to breath leads back to God. In John's Gospel the breath of Jesus has a divine quality about it. Jesus breathes on the apostles and says, "Receive the Holy Spirit" (Jn 20:22). Jesus breathing on the apostles is his bestowal of the Holy Spirit. Maximus the Confessor puts it quite simply, "God is breath."[7] Theophilus of Antioch says, "God has given to the earth the breath which feeds it. It is his breath that gives life to all things. And if he were to withhold his breath, everything would be annihilated. His breath vibrates in yours, in your voice. It is the breath of God that you breathe—and you are unaware of it."[8] One of the most moving uses of this metaphor comes from St. John of the Cross. "The soul that is united and transformed in God breathes God in God with the same divine breathing with which God, while in her, breathes her in himself."[9] Example after example bears witness to this tradition that uses breath as a metaphor of divine-human intimacy. But there is also a very practical aspect of this tradition: the use of one's own breath as a way to experience this divine-human intimacy, as an aid to dispel the illusion of separation from God.

One of the earliest Christian examples goes back possibly as far as the fourth century. Evagrius reputedly approached the famous monk, Macarius, and said, "Father, give me a word to live by." Macarius responds, "Secure the anchor rope to the rock and by the grace of God the ship will ride the devilish

waves of this beguiling sea." Macarius explained what he
meant: "The ship is your heart; keep guard over it. The rope is
your mind; secure it to our Lord Jesus Christ, who is the rock
who has power over all the waves ... because it is not difficult,
is it, to say with each breath, 'Our Lord Jesus, have mercy on
me: I bless thee, my Lord Jesus, help me?'"[10] If indeed this text
is as ancient as some believe it to be, it shows that from the
time when the teaching of contemplative practice begins to
be written down in the fourth century, there is an awareness
of the role of the breath in contemplative practice.[11] This monk
is advising Evagrius to say some form of the Jesus Prayer with
each breath. John Climacus, a seventh-century monk on Mount
Sinai says, "Let the remembrance of Jesus be with your every
breath. Then indeed you will appreciate the value of stillness."[12]

Following very much in the tradition of St. John Climacus,
another monk known as Hesychios, writes, "If you really wish
to cover over your evil thoughts,... to be still and calm, and to
watch over your heart without hindrance, let the Jesus Prayer
cleave to your breath, and in a few days you will find that this
is possible."[13] Elsewhere he says, "With your breathing combine watchfulness and the name of Jesus."[14] For Hesychios
incorporating the breath into one's contemplative practice can
help in the struggle with distracting thoughts and with establishing interior calm. Hesychios believes this will also lead
to wisdom and he recommends that we practice frequently
with the breath. "Let us live every moment in 'applying our
hearts to wisdom,' (Ps 90:12) as the Psalmist says, continually breathing Jesus Christ, the power of God the Father and
the wisdom of God" (1 Cor 1:24).[15] For Hesychios the pursuit
of wisdom involves practicing with the breath.

This tradition continues to be preserved and cultivated by the Orthodox tradition. In the fourteenth century at least three important figures advocate practicing with the breath. St. Gregory Palamas speaks most approvingly of the breath as an effective aid in calming a mind that is always darting about. In his work, *Those who Practice the Life of Stillness*, Palamas says it makes good sense and is especially useful for beginners, who might find the chaos of the mind a bit overwhelming. "That is why some teachers recommend them [beginners] to pay attention to the exhalation and inhalation of their breath, and to restrain it a little, so that while they are watching it the intellect, too, may be held in check."[16] Notice that the purpose of using the breath is quite straightforward: a simple aid to bringing stillness to the discursive mind. Moreover, he suggests, as others will do, "to restrain it a little." Presumably he means lengthening the exhalation. This aids the cultivation of calm and concentration. Who has not profited by advice to take a couple of deep breaths when overanxious? Interestingly Palamas does not mention combining the breath with the prayer word as others before him have done, though it would be hard to imagine that he would be opposed to this.

Nicephorus the Solitary, a monk of Mount Athos in Greece, likewise continues this tradition but with some interesting nuances. We spoke earlier of the heart as the symbol of that human depth that is deeper than thinking and feeling; this is where you discover yourself as already found by God. Nicephorus comes very much from this tradition. He has an understanding of the respiratory system, typical of the age, that sees air going from the lungs into the heart, and takes from this a model of contemplative practice. "And so, having collected your mind with you, lead it into the channel of breathing through which air reaches the heart and, together with this inhaled air, force your mind to descend into the heart and to remain there."[17] Nicephorus is not trying to turn us into spiritual contortionists. He is addressing something of great importance in any contemplative discipline: what do you do with your attention that is forever flitting about all over the place? He suggests giving the attention totally to the breath. As the breath leads air to the heart (according to his understanding of the respiratory system), so let the breath lead the attention into the spiritual heart that remains still in spite of whatever turbulence there may be in your thoughts and feelings.

Once the attention is stilled and steadied in this depth, then is the time to practice one's prayer word, which for him is the Jesus Prayer. "When your mind becomes fully established in the heart, it must not remain there silent and idle, but it should constantly repeat the prayer 'Lord, Jesus Christ, Son of God, have mercy upon me' and never cease."[18] It is worth noting a slight difference between the teaching of Nicephorus and that of John Climacus and Hesychios. Climacus and Hesychios suggest that from the beginning of a period of prayer, you combine your breathing with the prayer word. Nicephorus is slightly different. Use the breath to lead the attention into the heart, then begin the prayer word. The difference is of no great significance. What is important, however, is that all of these teachers advocate the use of the breath to cultivate interior stillness.

Near contemporaries of Nicephorus are two monks who wrote in collaboration, Callistus and Ignatius. In their *Directions to Hesychasts* they take on board the teaching of Nicephorus (in fact they cite the very passage from Nicephorus that we cited), but they too add some things of their own. They suggest breathing through the nose, "with closed lips,"[19] and not to let the attention focus on any thoughts or images, only on the Jesus Prayer. This will greatly facilitate the unification of the entire person. Importantly, Callistus and Ignatius emphasize that, however helpful the breath might be in prayer, the success of this "natural method" of prayer depends entirely on grace.[20] "The only reason why this method was invented by the holy fathers was to help collect thoughts, and to bring the mind from its usual dispersed flitting back to itself and to concentrate its attention."[21] Apart from all these observations and their emphasis on the centrality of grace in this practice, Callistus and Ignatius make it clear that they are handing on a Christian teaching on the role of the breath in contemplative practice that goes back many centuries.

After Callistus and Ignatius there crept in some suspicion regarding this tradition of practicing with the breath, and it is not entirely clear why. Theophan the Recluse (1815–1894) speaks with approval, "It is important to keep your consciousness in the heart, and as you do so to control your breathing a little so as to keep time with the words of the prayer."[22] Likewise Ignatii Brianchaninov (1807–1867) agrees that the strength of the attention can be aided by "quiet steady breathing."[23] However, they insist that working with the breath and other techniques, such as special postures and prostrations are not essential. In fact Ignatii Brianchaninov has heard of people damaging their lungs, and Theophan says that without suitable guidance it can be dangerous.[24] It is not entirely clear what Theophan and Ignatii are reacting to. The centuries-old tradition we have looked at is really quite simple: unite the Jesus Prayer with your breathing. Nicephorus, Callistus, and Ignatius consider it quite natural. Perhaps Theophan and Ignatii are seeing in the monasticism of their day a preoccupation with technique, which can derail the fruitful cultivation of any spiritual discipline. For example, we all know how easy it is for the attention to be stolen by the chaos of the wandering mind. Attention to the prayer word and breath can help recollect an otherwise riotous mind, but the seventeenth-century spiritual writer, Lorenzo Scupoli, seems overconcerned with technique when he says in his *Unseen Warfare* that the attention needs to be focused not on the breath but "just above the left nipple."[25] Undergraduates have found Scupoli's advice amusing; one asked if the nipple in question needed to be one's own! Common sense can usually spot misplaced emphasis.

The breath can be of real assistance in the deepening of contemplative practice. In fact the greater risk is not to use this important dimension of the body's wisdom. Shallow, short breathing is often resistance to deep, ungrasping stillness and can mask personal issues in the unconscious that have not been met. I would be quite prepared to guess that Mr. Duffy himself, living "a short distance from his body," had shallow, constricted breathing.

PRACTICING WITH THE BREATH

We have seen that the Christian tradition of using the breath as an aid to contemplation developed in the context of the Jesus Prayer tradition. But it can be used profitably with any prayer word or simply on its own. How then to make use of the breath during periods of prayer?

1. After assuming a stable posture, it is a good idea to take three or four very deep breaths. Breathe in deeply using the abdomen and exhale deeply. You don't want to be dramatic, but this does help clear the head and establish a firm

grounding in the present moment. The exhalation should be longer than the inhalation. St. Gregory of Sinai speaks of restraining the breath and suggests that it helps stabilize the mind.[26] This can be achieved by putting a *slight* brake on the exhalation. As some have put it, do it as though you have a feather on the end of your nose that you don't want to blow away during the exhalation. Then let your breath return to normal.

2. With the "breath held like a cap in the hand,"[27] now combine the prayer word with your breathing. If it is a single word, either on the inhale or the exhale. Some people say the word out loud, but most say it to themselves. If the prayer word is a phrase, such as the Jesus Prayer, recite half the phrase on the inhale and half on the exhale. The important thing is that the prayer word and the breath become one.

3. Let your attention rest gently but steadily on the breath as you breathe the prayer word. Eventually the attention, the breath, and the prayer word will form a unity. This will be your anchor in the present moment, a place of refuge and engaged vigilance.

4. Whenever you find that your attention has been stolen by thoughts, simply bring your attention back to the breathing of the prayer word. This is the simple practice. The practice is not "never let your attention be stolen." It will most definitely be stolen, perhaps every few seconds. The practice is to bring your attention back when you realize it has been stolen, whether it's every 30 seconds or every three seconds. The habit of gently returning to the present moment is what is being cultivated, and this habit gently excavates the present moment and cultivates dynamic stillness.

5. People often find that when they try to focus their attention on the breath they become uncomfortably self-conscious and begin to trip over themselves or feel that their breathing is forced. This is quite common, and it doesn't last too long; the self-consciousness is due to the newness of the practice. It is well worth putting up with this initial awkwardness. It will be gone in a matter of days. With time and practice the breath will deepen and drop from the upper chest to the abdomen. Three or four exhalations a minute is common. Here we see the really valuable contribution of the breath to contemplative practice. Those who discover the wisdom of the breath find it a great refuge that grounds the mental calm that contemplative practice cultivates. And we know that abdominal breathing contributes to health and a sense of well-being.

6. The wisdom of the breath is powerful. While there is no hard-and-fast rule that says attention to the breath must be worked into contemplative practice, it clearly adds depth to one's practice. From time to time I come across people with a real resistance to working with the breath. You need to be brutally honest with yourself regarding the nature of this resistance. Not infrequently I have found that those who could profit most by it have the strongest resistance to simply letting the attention rest on the breath. For example people who have strong mental habits of blaming others, resentment or who are hypersensitive to criticism often have hundreds of reasons why they can't possibly incorporate the breath into their practice. More often than not there are control issues here that tighten an egoic clamp on issues that are being kept from moving into consciousness. It is almost as though their survival

instinct tells them that the ego will be forced to unclench its fists if contemplative practice goes too deep.

The body is a great reservoir of wisdom. Something as simple as bodily stillness and breathing make a contribution of untold value to discovering the unfathomable silence deep within us. This silence, as R. S. Thomas tells us, "is when we live best, within listening distance of the silence we call God."[28]

FOUR

The Three Doorways
of the Present Moment:
The Way of the Prayer Word

Knock, and the door will be opened.
—*Matthew 7:7; Luke 11:9*

Enter eagerly into the treasure house that is within you and
you will see the things that are in heaven.
—*St. Isaac the Syrian*

The students always want to know whether or not Franny is pregnant. I've been teaching J. D. Salinger's *Franny and Zooey*, for some years now, and university undergraduates are intensely interested in her predicament. Salinger's ambiguity about Franny's possible pregnancy frustrates their desire to have things clearly spelled out for them, to have life clearly spelled out for them, to get closure on questions that must in the end be left open. They wrestle with this frustration more than they know, and it's not a bad context in which to situate the topic of the practice of silent prayer, which is a good deal closer to the heart of Salinger's book than whether or not Franny is pregnant.

Franny is in crisis. Her discovery of prayer is a major factor in this crisis. Both the unfolding of life and the unfurling of prayer have a way of keeping one on uncomfortably familiar terms with crisis, with the working out of our redemption. It is little wonder that the Christian story of this redemption also begins with a rather ambiguous pregnancy and a young Jewish woman who comes to know quite a lot about prayer and crisis and who "pondered these things in her heart" (Lk 2:19).

Franny is discovering how personal crisis bottoms out in prayer. She is sickened by the pretentious world of posturing in which she lives. She sees this pretense in those around her and she sees it in herself. She does not know what a tremendous grace it is that she can see this; nor does she realize that the ability to see her own self-centeredness, the sight of which has thrown her into crisis, is the fruit of her discovery of prayer. "I'm just sick of ego, ego, ego. My own and everybody else's," she tells Lane, her inattentive boyfriend. "I'm sick of it. I'm sick of not having the courage to be an absolute nobody. I'm sick of myself and everybody else that wants to make some kind of splash."[1] But she does sense that the "pea-green book" she carries with her, a copy of the Russian tale, *The Way of a Pilgrim*, contains something precious and vital that is holding her life together. Through *The Way of a Pilgrim* Franny is learning the Jesus Prayer, and the Jesus Prayer is making her into a real person, a person of prayer. The reader glimpses only the beginnings of this transformation.

What is the Jesus Prayer? It is an ancient way of praying that disposes the one who prays to the open depths within by drawing to stillness the wandering mind that flits and skitters all over the place. Normally our attention finds it difficult to be still; it is forever chasing the myriad thoughts with the result that there is a great deal of chatter going on in our heads. The Jesus Prayer, indeed any contemplative discipline, tries to interrupt this chatter. Instead of allowing the attention to be stolen yet again by our inner chatter, our attention is given a short phrase or word to quietly repeat, such as the Jesus Prayer: "Lord Jesus Christ, Son of God, have mercy on me" or quite simply the word "Jesus." The use of a prayer word or phrase to recollect the obsessive dimensions of the mind reaches far back in the Christian tradition.

THE PRAYER WORD

The prophetic voice of Isaiah announces the inner disposition of contemplative prayer. "You keep him in perfect peace whose mind is stayed on you" (see Is 26:3). In Mark's Gospel it is Jesus' mind that is stayed on one of his followers. Jesus meets the rich young man and is moved by his desire for eternal life. In a touching scene Jesus fixes his gaze on the rich young man. "Jesus looked steadily at him and he was filled with love for him." (Mk 10:21). Many contemplatives feel their prayer to be simplified to little more than allowing their awareness to rest in this mutual gazing announced by Isaiah and Mark. Our self-forgetful gaze on God is immersed in God's self-emptying gaze on us, and in this mutual meeting we find rest. John of the Cross came to define deep prayer along similar lines. "Preserve a loving attentiveness to God with no desire to feel or understand any particular thing concerning God."[2] By means of this loving attentiveness one begins to move into God.

In order for awareness to begin to drop its many scarves of self-consciousness and reveal its core—that overflowing vastness whose ground is God—we must first grow still. This is precisely where we meet the struggle of the human condition: we cannot be still. Even if the body can be still, the mind keeps racing like a runaway train. Our bodies may be at the place of prayer, but our minds are usually not where our bodies are, but instead are at a shopping mall; on a beach in Majorca; reliving an argument; fearing the future; regretting the past; any place but right here in the simplicity of the present moment.

The early contemplatives of the Egyptian desert knew all about this obsessive mental activity and knew how treacherously fragmenting it could be. They looked to Jesus' own encounter with Satan in the desert for an example of how to respond (Mt 4:1–11; Lk 4:1, 13). It was observed that when Jesus encountered Satan he refused to be drawn into conversation with Satan, choosing to quote Scripture rather than engage in conversation.[3] Satan says, "If you are the son of God, tell these stones to turn into loaves" (Mt 4:3). However, instead of reacting and getting caught up in dialogue, Jesus simply quotes Deuteronomy 8:3. "Human beings live not on bread alone but on every word that comes from the mouth of God" (Mt 4:4). When Satan says, "If you are the Son of God, throw yourself down" (Mt 4:6), Jesus again avoids getting drawn into conversation and simply quotes Scripture. "Do not put the Lord your God to the test" (Mt 4:7; see Dt 6:16). And so the encounter goes on until Jesus finally commands Satan to leave (Mt 4:10), or as Luke's version of the story puts it, "Having exhausted every way of putting him to the test, the devil left him, until the opportune moment" (Lk 4:13).

As the early contemplatives worked the example of Jesus into their own desert psychology, they realized the importance of not getting caught up in interior dialogues; for this gives way to the obsessive thinking that spells the ruin of inner peace, to say nothing of prayer. The demons could not enter the inner depths of the person. This was the Lord's domain. But the demons could exert considerable effort to keep us ignorant of these inner depths by bombarding us with whatever thoughts would most likely excite our patterns of obsession (the technical term for them is "the passions"). Once these obsessive patterns got going, the contemplative was thoroughly preoccupied by the flood of churning commentary that followed. Decade after decade, indeed a lifetime, can be spent in front of these videos.

The desert contemplatives saw this mind tripping all too clearly in their own lives and took to heart Jesus' example of refraining from inner dialogue with the afflictive thoughts. Instead of talking to yourself, recite, as Jesus did, a short phrase from Scripture. And so during periods of manual labor or solitary prayer, a short phrase, or a word was quietly repeated. An early example of this is found in St. Diadochos of Photiki. "When we have blocked all its outlets by means of the remembrance of God, the intellect requires of us imperatively some task which will satisfy its need for activity. For the complete fulfilment of its purpose we should give it nothing but the prayer 'Lord Jesus.' 'No one,' it is written, 'can say "Lord Jesus" except in the Holy Spirit' (1 Cor 12:3). Let the intellect continually concentrate on these words within its inner shrine with such intensity that it is not turned aside to any mental images."[4]

It is important to notice that it isn't a question of having no thoughts. Diadochos is aware that there is a dimension of the mind that is always doing something. So give it something to do: let it quietly repeat a short phrase. This is the specific purpose of the prayer word: to keep the attention from chasing thoughts and, once catching them, which it does with lightening-quick speed, whip up some commentary about the thought. Once you are aware that the attention has been stolen by a thought, simply bring your attention back. In the struggle with thoughts, the prayer word offers great assistance, bringing "every thought into captivity and obedience to Christ" (2 Cor 10:5). After seasons of practice, the fruit is the stillness, inner focus, and recollection of that dimension of human awareness that thinks, chatters, obsesses, and swarms like a plague of gnats. St. Augustine's vivid description of this in his Sermon on the Third Commandment, keeping holy the Sabbath, has the ring of personal experience:

> The third commandment enjoins quietness of heart, tranquility of mind. This is holiness. Because here is the Spirit of God. This is what a true holiday means, quietness and rest. Unquiet people recoil from the Holy Spirit. They love quarrelling. They love argument. In their restlessness they do not allow the silence of the Lord's Sabbath to enter their lives. Against such restlessness we are offered a kind of Sabbath in the heart. As if God were saying "Stop being so restless, quieten the uproar in your minds. Let go of the idle fantasies that fly around in your head." God is saying, "Be still and see that I am God" (Ps 46). But you refuse to be still. You are like the Egyptians tormented by gnats. These tiniest of flies, always restless, flying about aimlessly, swarm at your eyes, giving no rest. They are back as soon as you drive them off. Just like the futile fantasies that swarm in our minds. Keep the commandment. Beware of this plague.[5]

THE THREE DOORWAYS OF THE PRESENT MOMENT

When it comes to practicing with a prayer word or phrase such as the Jesus Prayer, the basic instruction couldn't be simpler: at the time of prayer let go of all other concerns, recollect yourself, and begin to repeat silently the prayer word. Whenever you become aware that your attention has been stolen, gently return your attention to the prayer word. Thus begins a journey to the depth of the present moment that can never be fully fathomed.

In what follows I shall speak of three doorways that must be passed through in order to discover this depthless depth within, but indeed I could have said 30 or 300 doorways, for they seem endless. But in truth there are no doorways. We should always be wary of applying linear notions of progress to our prayer life and asking ourselves: "What stage am I in?" "How far have I progressed?" Whatever "progress" in prayer is supposed to mean, it certainly doesn't work like that. This is something Thomas Merton pointed out toward the end of his life. He said, "In prayer we discover what we already have. You start from where you are and you deepen what you already have, and you realize you are already there. We already have everything but we don't know it and don't experience it. Everything has been given to us in Christ. All we need is to experience what we already possess."[6] There is nothing that separates us from this depthless depth whose ground is God. Paradoxically, however, this is only seen to be the case after crossing threshold after threshold. The present moment is a gateless gate opening onto a pathless path. Such are the paradoxes and riddles that pave the path of prayer.

It should likewise be emphasized that cultivating a contemplative practice, such as using a prayer word, the breath, sitting in stillness, is not to reduce prayer to a technique. Techniques imply a certain control and focus on a determined outcome. Contemplative practice is a skill, a discipline that facilitates a process that is out of one's direct control, but it does not have the capacity to determine an outcome. A gardener for example, does not actually grow plants. The gardener practices finely honed skills, such as cultivating soil, watering, feeding, weeding, pruning. But there is nothing the gardener can do to make the plants grow. However, if the gardener does not do what a gardener is supposed to do, the plants are not as likely to flourish. In fact they might not grow at all. In the same way a sailor exercises considerable skill in sailing a boat. But nothing the sailor does can produce the wind that moves the boat. Yet without the sailing skills that harness the wind, the boat will move aimlessly. Gardening and sailing involve skills of receptivity. The skills are necessary but by themselves insufficient. And so it is with contemplative practice and the spiritual life generally.

Contemplation is sheer gift. There is nothing we can do to bring forth its flowering, but there are important skills, without which it will be unlikely to flower. It is this sort of harmonious synergy between human effort and divine grace that leads St. Augustine to comment, "So while God made you without you, he doesn't justify you without you."[7] St. Teresa of Avila captures the same sense when she writes, "Beloved, there is much we can do to open ourselves to receiving his favors."[8] God is always Self-giving; it is a question of removing the obstacles that make it difficult to receive this Self-gift. This receptivity is what contemplative practice cultivates.

Teresa's famous image of the silk worm expresses what contemplative practice is for. As the silk worm spins its own silken cocoon, from which it will one day emerge transformed into a butterfly, so the soul, who gives itself diligently to spiritual practice, is responsive enough to the promptings of grace to cooperate in its own process of transformation.[9] Contemplative practice is like the cocoon that is gradually and delicately spun and from which we will emerge transformed. "So let's get on with it, my friends! Let's do the work quickly and spin the silken cocoon."[10]

THE FIRST DOORWAY

The First Doorway is characterized by largely practical concerns from general fidgetiness to boredom and self-preoccupation. Even experienced people of prayer can go through stretches of time when it is next to impossible to sit down and be physically still for 20 to 30 minutes a couple of times a day. But somehow we get there. The prayer word has a key role, especially for crossing the first doorway. As Diadochos indicated centuries ago, the prayer word provides an anchor, something to hold on to, to constantly return to, instead of the innumerable internal videos.

In the Christian tradition there is a wide variety of teaching regarding the use of the prayer word. The early desert tradition suggested the recitation of short scriptural phrases as a way of dealing with distracting thoughts. St. Augustine tells us that these were called "arrow prayers."[11] Evagrius has an amazing work called the *Antirrheticus*, in which he prescribes different scriptural phrases as antidotes for different types of distracting thoughts. He seems to advocate prayer phrases drawn directly from Scripture, and these in great variety, depending on the nature of the afflictive thought. For example, for those struggling with a particular form of anger he recommends, among others, such phrases as "'Do not quarrel along the way' (Gen 45:24) or 'Do not bear false witness against your neighbor'" (Ex 20:16).[12] If you are struggling with thoughts of sadness in some form, Evagrius suggests phrases

like, "'Therefore, if anyone is in Christ, he is a new creation'
(2 Cor 5:17) or 'Be not afraid before them, for I am with you
to deliver you, says the Lord'" (Jer 1:8).[13] The advantage of his
approach is that it cultivates several contemplative disciplines
at once: knowledge of Scripture, inner vigilance, and recollection. You have to be interiorly vigilant (and detached) in
order to identify immediately what facet of which thought is
afflicting you. You have also to be steeped in Scripture so that
the relevant scriptural phrases come immediately to mind.
Evagrius's intention is that the quiet repetition of these phrases
should gradually replace the obsessive chewing on the afflictive thoughts. The result is a therapeutic transformation of
our relationship with afflictive thoughts and feelings that sets
the tone for the entire contemplative tradition: afflictive
thoughts become opportunities for the cultivation of inner
stillness and immersion in Scripture.

While Evagrius teaches a great variety of prayer words tai-
lored to fit a variety of inner struggles, shortly after Evagrius,
this tradition is streamlined into a more measured array of
prayer words with a strong preference, at least in the Orthodox tradition, for some form of the Jesus Prayer.

Diadochos is an early spokesman of the Jesus Prayer tradition. The Jesus Prayer itself has long and short forms.
Diadochos and Climacus are among those who advocate a
short form of the prayer, that basically features "Jesus." As
the Jesus Prayer is handed on down the centuries, it takes on
longer forms: "Jesus Christ, Son of God, have mercy on me";
"Jesus Christ, Son of the living God, have mercy on me"; "Jesus
Christ, Son of the living God, have mercy on me, a sinner." In
my own experience of working with people from all walks of
life, some form of the Jesus Prayer is the most commonly used
of prayer phrases, but it is not the only one from the tradition.

The student of Evagrius, John Cassian, who brings much of the desert tradition into the West, suggests as a prayer phrase, "O God come to my assistance, O Lord make haste to help me" as part of his "prayer of fire."[14] This way of still prayer is for him the innermost reality and deepest praying of the "Our Father." Again we see a scripturally inspired way of silent prayer.

The anonymous author of *The Cloud of Unknowing* suggests a notably different approach to the prayer word. He thinks the prayer word should be brief. Nor should it have a lot of religious meaning; for this could then lead easily to pious reflection on the meaning of the prayer word. Therefore, he says, let it be a short word. "Take only a short word of one syllable; that is better than one of two syllables, for the shorter it is, the better it agrees with the work of the spirit. A word of this kind is the word 'God' or the word 'love.' Choose whichever you wish, or another as you please, whichever you prefer of one syllable, and fasten this word to your heart, so that it never parts from it, whatever happens."[15]

Either the author of *The Cloud* does not know of the Jesus Prayer tradition or he disagrees with its approach. But he does agree that the prayer word should become a place of constant refuge. In our own day there are two teachers who are particularly well known: Thomas Keating, who is largely inspired by the author of *The Cloud*, but from a helpful and contemporary psychological perspective, and John Main, who roots himself in the desert tradition. (However, his suggestion that the prayer word should be only "Maranatha," seems unique to him.)[16] So there is a good deal of diversity in the Christian tradition's teaching on the use of the prayer word. Nevertheless, there is a common concern that unites this diversity: the acknowledged problem of the roving mind in prayer and the usefulness of the prayer word as a remedy.

You might well ask, isn't the mental repetition of a word or phrase just another video? Yes, it is in a certain sense. There is something discursive about it. But this will take care of itself in passing through the third doorway. The prayer word is something like a vaccination: a small dose of the disease in question is introduced to the patient for the purpose of calling forth those antibodies that will ultimately ward off the disease. In this case the disease in question is the overactive mind, which, while undeniably important in many of life's tasks, obscures the deeper ground of being and leaves us with the sense that we are separate from God and others. This sense of separation from God, as well as the sense of personal identity derived from thoughts and feelings, is all pasted up out of bits and pieces of mental process.

The vaccine of the prayer word builds recollection and detachment. Recollection gives us an initial sense of inner peace, which will lead to a yet deeper calm, grounding both inner peace and inner chaos (what the desert tradition calls *apatheia*). Detachment is another dynamic quality that enables us to let go of things and to see through our endless and clever mind games.

Choose a prayer word and stick with it. Some people seem to get a spiritual buzz out of choosing their prayer word. It needn't be so involved; simply choose a word that you feel drawn to or that seems right and leave it at that.

The challenge most people face in passing through the first doorway is coping, on the one hand, with the tremendous noise going on in the head, and, on the other, with paralyzing boredom. The mind seems to be darting about with a great and furious frenzy. Simply note this and then return to your prayer word. It is not a question of trying to push the chaotic thoughts away and replacing them with peaceful thoughts; for this would be yet another way of getting caught up in more thinking. Simply return to the prayer word. We might well catch ourselves commenting, "This is a hopelessly boring and inane practice." These are more thoughts. The advice is the same: note them; let them be; return to the prayer word. This simple discipline is called "practice."

Sometimes, especially at the beginning, there can be a lot of self-consciousness that can really trip us up. We either become fascinated by watching ourselves being contemplative or find this self-consciousness too awkward and distracting. The advice is the same: note the thoughts, let them be, and return to the practice.

The skill that is being cultivated in all this is what is needed to pass through the first doorway. This skill is really a sort of mental habit: we are becoming accustomed to returning to our practice in the midst of whatever is happening, whether things are going well or whether all hell is breaking loose. This habit of constantly returning to our practice is more than just a mechanical repetition. Theophan says in reference to the practice of the Jesus Prayer, "Do not forget that you must not limit yourself to a mechanical repetition of the words of the Jesus Prayer. This will lead to nothing but a habit of repeating the prayer automatically. . . . There is of course nothing wrong with this, but it constitutes only the extreme outer limit of the work."[17] The practice of the prayer word involves more than just fidelity to technique. "Its power comes from faith in the Lord, and from a deep union of the mind and heart with Him."[18] When we find that this practice is really beginning to take root in us, that this is how we increasingly spend our time when the reasoning mind is not needed for some task, that we spend less and less time watching our internal videos, then we have passed through the First Doorway of the present moment. It is a subtle yet obvious passage, something like what happens to a pianist when learning a new piece of music. At first it is awkward, stumbling and halting, but with practice, practice, and more practice, suddenly it becomes natural. The awkwardness of self-consciousness is gone; the prayer word is becoming a place of refuge, and somehow quantity has become quality, as Franny put it in *Franny and Zooey*.[19]

The Second Doorway

When negotiating the Second Doorway the main task is to become one with the prayer word, the way a weaver is one with the loom, or a dancer with the dance. Returning to the prayer word has become second nature and is refreshingly more interesting than the internal videos that continue to play. Certainly the attention will be stolen by the videos but bringing ourselves back to our practice is now well established. And so we forget ourselves in the prayer word.

Previously the prayer word was like a brick wall, and the quiet repetition of it involved a good deal of mental activity. This begins to change as we approach the Second Doorway. The repetition of it is far less a mental saying and more a part of our simple awareness.

We may also become aware of some of the physical and emotional benefits that often accompany a well-established contemplative practice. Many people find that blood pressure decreases or stabilizes, the pulse slows down, and there is greater emotional tone. Life will continue to bring its stresses and strains, but we are more aware of how we are the cause of much of our own suffering and, in any event, can somehow let go with greater facility. We get over things more quickly.

There is a certain wisdom that settles into a life that does not attempt to control what everybody else ought to be thinking, saying, doing, or voting on. Wisdom, health, life, and love cannot be found in trying to control the wind, but rather in harnessing the wind in the sails of receptive engagement of the present moment. The most searching example of doing just this is quite simply to return to our practice rather than indulge in yet another video, yet another strategy of control. This ability is a result of deepening interior silence and makes it easier to give ourselves entirely to the praying of the prayer word.

Theophan says that practicing with a prayer word is more than something mechanical. "Delve deeply into the Jesus Prayer, with all the power that you possess."[20] While the Jesus Prayer is Theophan's prayer word, the dynamic I describe, the fruit of interior silencing, works with any contemplative practice that cultivates recollection (as well as for those who find themselves closer to John of the Cross and simply sit in loving awareness, without the assistance of a prayer word). Theophan says, "delve deeply." He has become aware of the prayer word's attractive quality. This depthless depth must be plumbed.

No effort on our part can make the Second Doorway open, but the various skills cultivated at this time are necessary in order to cross the threshold of the Second Doorway, once opened by grace and providence. The skills we learn in our practice are letting go, letting be, and living in the depth of the present moment. A generous amount of time given each day to the practice of the prayer word is the best way to facilitate this process.

The struggle with thoughts has been present from the beginning. But after crossing the threshold of the First Doorway there are some subtler dimensions of this struggle with thoughts that entail the purification of the grasping tendencies of the discursive mind.

The thinking mind dominates awareness with clenching fists that constantly search for something to grasp. Contemplation, by contrast requires open palms of simple, direct engagement. This grasping tendency of the mind is the subject of the healing, purification, and unification that will help it remain still and receptive.

Before the First Doorway, the prayer word functioned much as shield or place of refuge. We could see that a thought had stolen our attention and then we returned to the prayer word. As we approach the Second Doorway, the prayer word is steadying our gaze on something more subtle: the obsessive mental patterns that are shaping and driving the thoughts and feelings that steal the attention. Say, for example, we are struggling with thoughts of anger or resentment. As we approached the First Doorway we gained the ability to see when the attention had been stolen by angry thoughts. As we approach the Second Doorway the stillness of the prayer word allows not only the resentful thought to be spotted, but also the mental-emotional pattern that undergirds the thought. We can see ourselves whipping up a commentary on past hurts that angered or frightened us. The commentary happens when the mind uses one of its millions of hands to grab onto something (real or imagined). This grabbing, and it is lightening quick, produces the story we tell ourselves about our anger, this is what resentment is. It is crucial to be able to spot these stories, for there will be no liberation until we learn to drop the elaborate commentaries on our anger, and we cannot drop them until we can see ourselves doing it. As the practice of the prayer word leads us to deeper interior silence, we can calmly see this spinning of stories in our head in a way we never could before.

Theophan says the prayer word "will draw you together."[21] One of the effects of the integration of our emotions into the prayer word is that we can now see the deeper patterns of mental obsession and grasping that shape and drive afflictive thoughts and feelings. This liberating and integrating dynamic characterizes the approach to the Second Doorway. It can be rather painful as repressed material comes into awareness, what Thomas Keating has called "the unloading of the unconscious."[22] But this is the essence of liberating integration: allowing into awareness what was previously kept out of awareness. Until we can see this, we will not see that there is something utterly vast and sacred already within us, this silent land that runs deeper than these obsessive mental patterns.

The use of the prayer word at the First Doorway of practice is characterized by the effective use of the prayer word as a refuge or shield from the onslaught of thoughts, even pious thoughts. It isn't that the prayer word prevents thoughts from happening, but we can use it to help us from getting caught up in them. As we cross the threshold of the Second Doorway, however, the way the prayer word is used begins to change. The deeper we delve into the prayer word, the less we use it as a shield from afflictive thoughts. Rather we meet the thoughts with stillness instead of commentary. We let the thoughts simply be, but without chasing them and whipping up commentaries on them.

As important as using the prayer word as a refuge and shield had been at the First Doorway, there was still a running mental commentary that said something like "I can't have this thought." "I must let go of thoughts." An independent "I" exists who has objective thoughts that must be let go. This is very much how things look from the First Doorway. The problem with this, however, is that there is still a separation between you and the prayer word. But as the prayer word continues to facilitate inner unification, this self-conscious, independent "I" dominates less and less. As the threshold of the Second Doorway is crossed the commentary that says "I can't have this thought" goes, and we are no longer meeting thoughts as afflictions to be shielded from and deflected. Instead the prayer word allows us to meet thoughts with simple stillness instead of a commentary such as "I need to let go of that thought."

Theophan says, "Have no intermediate image between the mind and the Lord when practicing the Jesus Prayer."[23] When we are not grasping at the thoughts, images, and commentaries that separate us from the prayer word, we are one with the prayer word. The prayer word has gradually changed from being like a shield of protection to being like a riverbed at one with the river. The riverbed makes no comment on what is coming from upstream and passing downstream. Receiving and letting go are one act. This is how we come to experience the steady flow of thoughts and feelings.

Having passed through the Second Doorway, many people find that they no longer need to repeat the prayer word or, if so, only infrequently. While some schools of Christian meditation may teach otherwise, it seems to me completely natural for the prayer word to go completely silent after the Second Doorway. It is perfectly appropriate to emphasize constant repetition of the prayer word before the First Doorway is crossed. But even here the prayer word's main purpose is simply to bring the attention back from chasing thoughts and thereby assist the gentle excavation of the present moment. While constant repetition of the prayer word is nevertheless useful training, Theophan reminds us that "the words are only the instrument and not the essence of the work."[24] The more silent we become the more silent the prayer word; the fewer thoughts separating us from the prayer word, the more we have become one with the prayer word.

As we cross the Second Doorway we somehow become aware of our primordial foundation in silence. The prayer word, whether mentally repeated or not, leaves a trace in awareness, a traceless trace that serves as a vehicle of this silence. Merely turning our attention to the presence of the prayer word reveals this immersion in silence in which all thoughts appear and disappear. The prayer word is effectively practiced by *just being*. Here we wait for the Third Doorway to open.

THE THIRD DOORWAY

Crossing the threshold of the Third Doorway requires vigilant waiting in the silence of just being. When we are well practiced in this way of prayer we will find that we have acquired a certain skill at recognizing thoughts. They appear and disappear in awareness. Now shift your attention from the thought to what is aware of the thought, the awareness itself. This is a very simple shift, but a shift that immediately reveals (however briefly) the still mind. The discursive, reasoning mind will immediately try to turn this too into an object of awareness by generating a mental image of the stillness or a thought such as "the mind is now still" and then embroider some commentary on that. But by now we are well aware of the subtlety of our thoughts. We have learned to use the prayer word as a refuge from these thoughts. We have learned to meet thoughts with stillness instead of obsessive commentary that we play over and over and over again. So now shift your attention from these objects of awareness to the *aware-ing* itself. The prayer word is essentially silent at this point, even if at more surface levels of consciousness it might be quietly recited. Here one waits, and when the moment is ripe the present moment opens up.

Crossing the Third Doorway we encounter the ineffable. It is ineffable because it is neither an "it" nor a "what." It is nothing that can be grasped by thoughts, feelings, words. Language wilts. The prayer word opens. It reveals not another object of awareness, but the groundless ground that is the core of all being. This typically registers to the mind as an indescribable vastness, streaming from all sides, streaming from no sides, an ocean full and overflowing with a luminous nothing. But I am not describing some particular thing that appears as an object of awareness, as some sort of visual or sensible experience, something you see happening to you. I'm trying to point to where no word has ever gone, but out of which the Word emerges. And so this Silence washes onto the shores of perception, making it stretch to receive in metaphors of light, union, calm, spaciousness.

The very attention that gazes into this vastness is itself this vastness, luminous depth gazing into luminous depth. You are the vastness into which you gaze. "Deep calls unto deep in the roar of your waters" (Ps 42:7). But we must come to know this for ourselves as we are carried through this doorway of unknowing into the silent land.

One of the characteristics of having moved through the Third Doorway shows itself in our sense of self. On the one hand a firm, quiet confidence in our identity replaces all the posturing and masquerading. At the same time we discover that concepts, language, images, feelings do not exhaust or adequately express who we are; they don't go as deep as we go. Even a notion such as "you" or "I" falls short. Most of what we call a "self" is seen to be a paste-up job. The paste-up job, what many call the ego, has its use for negotiating all the practical affairs of life and is of no little interest to the Enneagram, the medicine man, the tax man. But no label applies to this "unselfed self" who emerges from the Third Doorway.[25]

This is not the loss of identity, but its flowering, and we inhale the perfume of a fundamental Christian truth that baptism proclaims: my "I am" is one with Christ's "I am." In the language of traditional theology, we move from image to likeness (Gen 1:26). St. Diadochos reminds us that we are all "made in God's image; but to be in His likeness is granted only to those who through great love have brought their own freedom into subjection to God. For only when we do not belong to ourselves do we become like Him who through love has reconciled us to Himself."[26] This "not belonging to ourselves" of which Diadochos speaks is our identity in God, the core of who we are. Thoughts do not attach to it. Time does not touch it. Yet it embraces all thought, all time, our coming to birth, and our dying. It is what the prophet Jeremiah calls our self before we were born and known by God from all eternity: "Before I formed you in the womb I knew you" (Jer 1:5) or St. Paul's acclamation in his letter on freedom, "I live now not with my own life but with the life of Christ who lives in me" (Gal 2:20).

People have often used the language of light to describe this breakthrough into the utterly normal. It is dark to the discursive mind but light to the virtues and to the awakening contemplative faculties. St. Gregory of Nyssa calls it a "luminous darkness." Again St. Diadochos speaks for many when he refers to this breakthrough as seeing "the light of the mind." He understands this as the fruit of long concentration on the prayer word (for him the name of Jesus). "Those who meditate unceasingly upon this glorious and holy name in the depths of their heart can sometimes see the light of their own intellect."[27] Diadochos is not speaking of some sort of vision or appearance of physical light, some form that could then disappear, much less some image of God, which could only be stitched together out of concepts and images. John of the Cross uses this same imagery when he says to God, "You are the divine light of my intellect by which I can look at You."[28] The "light of the mind" is a metaphor for the ground of awareness showing something of itself to our perception. Something of the groundless ground of God washes onto the shores of perception and registers as spaciousness, luminous vastness, a sense of the unity of all things, a sense of everything manifesting vastness, what the poet Geoffrey Hill calls "splendidly shining darkness ... emptiness ever thronging."[29] It is marked by a sense of deep inner freedom, even in the midst of all sorts of constraints, limitations, trials, failings, and responsibilities.

The prayer word has served as a vehicle for this breakthrough. Once this breakthrough has integrated us into itself, has "made our thoughts captive to Christ" (2 Cor 10:5), we realize something far more precious than any jewel. This luminous ground of God, is the ground that upholds all creation, "the Love that moves the sun and the other stars" as Dante put it,[30] the depths of our own heart, awareness itself utterly steeped in and saturated by God. Here we move into the promised land, the self-forgetful consummation in silence of our created identity, transformed from image to likeness (Gen 1:26), manifestly hidden "with Christ in God" (Col 3:3).

Whether we continue to repeat the prayer word or not is relevant only insofar as the discursive mind needs some steadying. In any case, it is not uncommon, especially if you use the Jesus Prayer, to continue feeling a certain devotion, reverent gratitude or sense of the sacred with respect to the prayer word. Each person may differ here, but after the Third Doorway is crossed, contemplative practice is mainly a silent and uncluttered gazing into luminous vastness that streams out as our own awareness, a riverbed of awareness in which all things appear and disappear.

Using a prayer word is more than mere technique. The prayer word is like a mirror that reflects our own awareness. When we first begin the inward turn to quiet prayer we are faced with chaos, and the prayer word serves as an anchor in a storm, a shield and refuge from the onslaught of thoughts, feelings, storms of boredom, and fidgeting. But with some practice with the prayer word we grow in recollection and concentration and begin to see that there is something deeper than the chaos within. And somehow the prayer word seems different from before; it is as though there is some depth to it and Theophan's advice to "delve deeply" into it makes sense. The doorways we begin to pass through are doorways into our own awareness, our own inner depths where we meet in this luminous darkness the gracious God who is already shining out of our own eyes, "closer to me than I am to myself."

What precisely is the prayer word doing? The prayer word gently excavates the present moment. The resulting interior focus eventually sets off and maintains a process of interior silencing. This interior silencing in turn begins to clear away much of the noise in our head. We discover in the process that there is more depth within us than we ever dreamt. There is not only chaos, confusion, emotional attachment, anxiety, and anger's nettled memory; not just the marvel of discursive reason, imaginative insight, and unconscious instinct, but also an abyss of awareness that is always flowing with bright obscurity, grounding all these mental processes, one with all and one with God. The prayer word assists this excavation of the present moment until such time as the prayer word too falls silent. Ultimately all strategies of spiritual acquisition become silent and our practice, if it can be called that any more, is simply luminous vastness gazing on and gazed through by luminous vastness.

However, just because we have crossed the threshold of the Third Doorway, does not mean we don't go back and forth. These doors are double-hinged, and we can go back and forth quite a bit. Sometimes when life is particularly stormy we may well find ourselves practicing as though we were approaching the First Doorway for the first time. We can even feel resistance to sitting in silence at all. But once the Third Doorway has been crossed, the time spent knocking on previous doors diminishes, and we see that even the resistance to sitting in silence is minimal.

The discovery of this mystery of silence is the grace of a lifetime, the "pearl of great price." The best response to this grace is to gather in the folds of this mantle of silence and wrap them around us. Concretely this means frequent practice. Just as we cannot expect to be in good health by eating a nutritious meal once a week or to be physically fit by walking around the block once a month, so it is with contemplative practice. Like physical health and fitness the fruits of contemplative practice are seen in regular practice. St. Diadochos reminds us that anyone "who merely practices the remembrance of God from time to time, loses through lack of continuity what he hopes to gain through his prayer."[31] Regular daily practice is key.

Thomas Keating recommends 20-minute periods twice a day. This is good for establishing a practice. If just starting out, this may seem too much. Then try eight or ten minutes and slowly increase to 20. But I would recommend gradually building up to 30 minutes to an hour twice a day. Most people find the morning the most realistic time for prayer. Others find evening or before bed better. The general rule is that the best time is what allows for the most consistency day in and day out. It takes real commitment to create a workable routine. One contemplative has defined contemplation as "the art of stealing time."

But as important as time set aside specifically for prayer, is learning to sit when you are not sitting. By this I mean, whenever the reasoning mind is not required for a specific task, take this as an opportunity to practice. Commuting to and from work, shopping for groceries, showering, shaving, cooking, ironing, gardening. All of these tasks, and others, are perfectly workable with contemplative practice and the principles of common sense. Far from lulling the reasoning mind into some dull blankness, contemplative practice sharpens reason and engenders all manner of creativity. So there is no cause for concern here. The bottom line is this: minimize time given over to chasing thoughts, dramatizing them in grand videos, and believing these videos to be your identity. Otherwise life will pass you by.

With so much focus on contemplative practice and interior stillness, what about other forms of prayer? Do they simply disappear? This does happen. But it is simply because a deeper discovery has been made. By sheer grace of God, our very being itself is prayer. Heaping up prayer upon prayer makes about as much sense as writing a chatty Valentine's Day card to your beloved when your beloved is with you. There is still an important role for intercessory prayer, but don't be surprised if you discover that silent communion with the ground of all being becomes the most natural and simple way of being in solidarity with all humanity and holding all our needs before the Creator of all.

Community prayer remains important, but how you participate in it changes. Liturgical prayer has a way of becoming a fountain of grace. The flow of this sourceless source is nothing other than the visible form of the great self-emptying sacramental flow of the ground of being. In former times it was common to speak of the liturgy on earth as a reflection of the liturgy in heaven. We don't speak of liturgy this way any more, but this point of view makes more and more sense. For when we enter these doorways of silence the simplest truths of the liturgy are unveiled: liturgy, like creation itself, is the shimmering of eternity in time. Even in the most dismal of liturgies (and these are in no short supply) Christ is and has always been the only presider.

However, just because we come to intuit this as the simplest truth about liturgical prayer, this does not necessarily mean that it is easy to cope with large doses of liturgy. The Benedictine monk John Chapman, has something rather sobering to say about this. In his classic *Spiritual Letters* he says, "It is common enough for those who have any touch of 'Mysticism' . . . to be absolutely unable to find any meaning in vocal prayers."[32] Chapman is not devaluing prayers we say privately or in common. He is putting his finger on a problem many contemplatives face. We find it difficult to pray with words. Communal prayer itself is not the issue. Contemplative prayer is the prayer of *just being*. Sadly much liturgical prayer is often hopelessly cerebral, self-conscious, verbose, and distracted (to say nothing of having all those bits of paper waved in your face). This is no environment in which simplicity can easily flower. Each will have to negotiate these tensions for oneself.

The way of the Christian prayer word is a way of liberation. By the time the Second Doorway is crossed, we begin to see some of the effects of this liberation. There is an increasing tendency to encounter life in its varied, concrete simplicity—however it happens to be—as simply a manifestation of the ineffable luminous vastness. This is marked by improved psychological hygiene. Life still hurts, but our emotional tone is such that we get over things quicker and on the whole our pet obsessions aren't quite the same easily hooked nose rings as before.

Part of the reason for this liberation is that all sorts of projections have been withdrawn. Prior to the major breakthrough of the Third Doorway our sense of self is highly mediated and is reflected back to us as a deep attraction to the things we think we need in order to discover our true selves. And so we burn with desire to spend time in spiritual places. We think we have to enter a monastery to realize our true self. We think the perfect spouse will lead us to the discovery of ourselves. We think that our true self is something that can be acquired and we burn with zealous desire to acquire it. But as our gaze into the luminous vastness deepens and strengthens, and the prayer word grows quiet, and spiritual practices fall away due to their own ripened readiness, so do our projections onto monasteries, cathedrals, canyons, mountains, and the "perfect partner" also fall away. When we discover unshakably that the God we seek has already found us, then the "monastery" or "mountain" or "perfect partner" does not have the same pull. They are no longer holding out to us a reflection of our inner-most self that is one with God. Our self hidden with Christ in God (Col 3:3) is bodying forth as life-just-happening. We don't have to enter or leave the monastery in order to discover this; we don't have to enter or leave the monastery after discovering this. The all-reconciling silence of God, resounding in all sound, is the parting gift of the prayer word. "The heavens declare the glory of God, the vault of heaven proclaims his handiwork. . . . No utterance at all, no speech, no sound that anyone can hear; yet their voice goes out through all the earth, and their message to the ends of the world" (Ps 19:1–4).

FIVE

The Riddles of Distraction

The proverbs of Solomon son of David, king of Israel: for learning... the sayings of the sages and their riddles.

—Proverbs 1:1–6

Once the master of the house has got up and locked the door, you may find yourself standing outside knocking on the door, saying "Lord, open to us," but he will answer, "I do not know where you come from."

—Luke 13:25

Look, I am standing at the door, knocking.

—Revelation 3:2

I am the door.

—John 10:9

The doorways of the present moment are each guarded by an elaborately simple array of distractions that works in tandem with the prayer word. Together they open the doorways into the silent land. These distractions are like riddles that must first be answered before the door will open. The riddles, however, are not answered by the calculating mind but by successive silences. These silences are built around a central paradox: all distractions have within them the silent depths we seek, the flowing vastness of Presence that eludes every grasp of comprehension. Therefore, distractions do not have to be rid of in order for them to relax their grip and reveal their hidden treasure. Such is the simplicity of paradox.

The various riddles of distraction are more or less related to the doorway we are entering. However, from the perspective of contemplative practice it doesn't really matter what the content of the distractions is (though this may be of psychotherapeutic interest). The content of distractions will vary greatly. It could be the trivial sort of chattering to ourselves about work, shopping, planning meals, refiguring the budget, or it could be more afflictive struggles with personal pain, grief, brokenness, resentment, fear. What is important is how we meet distraction. This will be my focus. How we meet distraction (not whether or not we experience distractions—this is a given) is what heals and transforms as we move deeper. We may experience mere mental chatter or we may struggle with real afflictions, but to what extent these are distracting will change depending on how we meet these distractions that appear in the valley of our awareness.

The distractions we encounter are the riddles of Solomon's sages (Prov 1:5): they teach us, they train us, and they hold out to us the following riddles. First, are you your thoughts and feelings? Second, what do thoughts and feelings appear in? Third, what is the nature of these thoughts and feelings, and who is aware of them? Again, these riddles are not answered by our reason but by our own inner silence. We can study endless maps of the pathways into the silent land. But the map is not the territory. To discover the actual land of silence requires not information but the silence of God that is the very ground of the mind and that causes us to seek in the first place. When the distractions of each doorway call forth from us the required silence, then the distractions will have served their purpose, and the door will open.

Distraction serves a purpose. Like gargoyles guarding the roofline of a cathedral, distractions first serve to ward off those who lack proper motivation. In an age when people claim to be "spiritual, not religious"—not really knowing what they mean by either—lack of proper motivation is common. We must long for truth, freedom, loving communion with the silent depths of God. In the strange way that common sense is not very common, many people would rather win an argument than know liberating truth or would rather feel safe than discover what it means to live in freedom under grace (Rom 6:14). If we do not want truth, freedom, God, distractions will cause the door to appear closed.

THE RIDDLE OF THE FIRST DOORWAY:
ARE YOU YOUR THOUGHTS AND FEELINGS?

The riddles of the First Doorway are real tangles of distraction. Their primary purpose is to pry us away from one of the fundamental traps of the spiritual journey: identification with our thoughts and feelings. If we think we are our thoughts and feelings, we go through life simply reacting to what is going on around us, with little awareness that we are even doing this or that life could be otherwise. When we try to pray, distractions will strike us as being especially ensnaring, even overwhelming. When we try to sit still there is very little sense that there is anything within us other than these videos that constantly play. But usually we are so caught up in them that we do not even notice them, and yet our lives are completely scripted by them. The cocktail party going on in our head is our life.

Distraction at the First Doorway is characterized by this complete identification with thoughts and feelings. When we sit in prayer in the midst of all this, it can be quite an ordeal. For example, we are trying to sit in silence with our prayer word, and the people next door start blasting their music. Our mind is so heavy with its own noise that we actually hear very little of the music. We are mainly caught up in a reactive commentary: "Why do they have to have it so loud!" "I'm going to phone the police!" "I'm going to sue them!" And along with this comes a string of emotional commentary, crackling irritation, and spasms of resolve to give them a piece of your mind the next time you see them. The music was simply blasting, but we added a string of commentary to it. And we are completely caught up in this, unaware that we are doing much more than just hearing music. The example might seem a bit of an exaggeration; the point is that this sort of ensnarement by thought upon thought upon thought, all a mass of blaring music, typifies how we encounter distractions at the First Doorway.

Or say we are sitting in prayer, and someone whom we don't especially like or perhaps fear enters the room. Immediately we become embroiled with the object of fear, avoiding the fear itself, and we begin to strategize: perhaps an inconspicuous departure or protective act of aggression or perhaps a charm offensive, whereby we can control the situation by ingratiating ourselves with the enemy. The varieties of posturing are endless, but the point is that we are so wrapped up in our reaction, with all its commentary, that we hardly notice it happening, though we feel the bondage.

The problem at this early phase is that as we pray we meet what is happening (and distractions are part of what is happening) with commentary instead of stillness. All this reactive chatter prevents the simple, direct experience of our thoughts and emotions and increases suffering immeasurably and unnecessarily. This is why most people do not stick with a contemplative discipline for very long; we have heard all sorts of talk about contemplation delivering inner peace but when we turn within to seek this peace, we meet inner chaos instead of peace. But at this point it is precisely the meeting of chaos that is salutary, not snorting lines of euphoric peace. The peace will indeed come, but it will be the fruit, not of pushing away distractions, but of meeting thoughts and feelings with stillness instead of commentary. This is the skill we must learn.

The struggle with distractions is not characterized only by afflictive thoughts. Many sincerely devout people never enter the silent land because their attention is so riveted to devotions and words. If there is not a wordy stream of talking to God and asking God for this and that, they feel they are not praying. Obviously this characterizes any relationship to a certain extent. When we are first getting to know someone, the relationship is nurtured by talking. Only with time does the relationship mature in such a way that we can be silent with someone, that silence comes to be seen to be the deeper mode of communion. And so it is with God; our words give way to silence.

The reason this doorway requires so much patience is that our awareness is so freighted with thinking. Whenever we turn within we meet chatter, thinking, and commenting. In consequence, while we are aware of spiritual longing, we perceive ourselves to be cut off from the deeper ground of our being, where the Silence of the Word is forever emptying itself out in being-as-creation, the way a vine extends into branches (cf. Jn 15:5). The ground of who we are is completely porous, porous as a sponge immersed in what flows through it. But because the awareness is so freighted with thinking, and the attention so riveted to the thinking and the chatter, awareness as simple, spacious immersion in God gets refracted as the search for God-as-object-to-be-acquired. We all start out here, but it is a highly filtered perception of things. Theologians should be aware that this is not a question of a metaphysical blurring of Creator and creature. It is a question of the transfiguration of awareness, the consummation in silence of grace's initiative in creation, baptism, and eucharist.

The prayer word is of great assistance in answering the riddle of the First Doorway. While the First Doorway doesn't require the depth of silence that others will, the prayer word here helps to soften our reactive response of inner chatter and calms our tendency to react to thoughts and feelings by tackling them with still more thoughts and feelings. By cultivating our practice with the prayer word we learn to face thoughts and feelings directly instead of reacting to them. This is the first of the successive silences we must learn. When we learn to return to the prayer word instead of reacting to the videos and chatter, and truly find refuge in the prayer word, even if thoughts are annoying us, then we will have answered the riddle of distraction that guards the First Doorway.

THE RIDDLE OF THE SECOND DOORWAY:
WHAT DO THOUGHTS AND FEELINGS APPEAR IN?

The riddle of the Second Doorway is notably different from that of the First. At the First Doorway we are completely, or nearly completely, caught up in and dominated by our reactions. After the First Doorway we become much more aware of what is happening within. One of the fruits of interior silence is precisely this growth in awareness. Growth does not mean that somehow we are no longer going to struggle with our issues. Much struggle remains with us for a very long time. But what does change is how we experience the struggle. We are able to see with greater clarity what is going on within us as it is happening. We move from being a victim of what is happening to being a witness to what is happening. Things keep happening, but we experience them differently. This move from victim to witness is an early psychological fruit of the contemplative journey. It is deeply liberating and gives us a sense of possibility for real change in our lives. People often comment that this growth in awareness of thoughts and feelings, *simply letting them be*, is something their therapists have been trying to get them to do for years. They could not do this before, because they were too caught up in reacting to thoughts and feelings and acting out of them. They had not cultivated the interior discipline that enabled them to make this shift from victim to witness.

Awareness is the eye of silence. The riddle of the Second Doorway helps us deepen this silence by training the attention not to spin commentary on the thoughts and feelings that we become aware of. This was one of the principle aims of the contemplative training in the desert tradition, and Evagrius is the real master here. He was aware that the attempt to be silent involved one immediately in the struggle with thoughts. He could see the difference between the mere presence of a thought and something within us (he called it a passion) that seized the thought and whipped it up into a frothy, obsessive commentary. These obsessive patterns within us generate anxiety, suffering, and the sense of restless isolation from God and others.

Evagrius is not telling us not to have these thoughts; for the attempt to have no thoughts simply produces more thoughts. As Teresa of Avila would put it centuries later, "The harder you try not to think of anything, the more aroused your mind will become and you will think even more."[1] Much less does Evagrius want us to run from thoughts or to suppress them; this would be more mental commentary on them. His advice is to turn the tables on all this chatter and simply observe without commenting. Observe everything about the thoughts. "Let him keep careful watch over his thoughts. Let him observe their intensity, their periods of decline and follow them as they rise and fall. Let him note well the complexity of his thoughts, their periodicity, the demons which cause them, with the order of their succession and the nature of their associations."[2] Evagrius wants us to know what presses our buttons, what gets us going. Who winds us up? Under what conditions? Does hunger make you have a shorter fuse? Does a short temper mask a sense of being threatened? Is struggle with shame really pride inside out? When are we more susceptible to these afflictive thoughts? Do they repeat? Do they follow a pattern? How long do they last? What other thoughts do they team up with? Evagrius thinks it is essential that we know all about these torturous thoughts, "so that when these various evil thoughts set their own proper forces to work we are in a position to address effective words against them, that is to say, those words which correctly characterize the one present."[3] If we can name the thought (anger, fear, pride, etc.) instead of spinning a commentary *about* the thought, which is our usual response, we stand a much better chance of simply letting go of the thought and returning to our practice. Initially this can be rather laborious; for there might be some basic self-knowledge that needs to be acquired, sometimes requiring the assistance of a therapist. However, most people who are drawn to the contemplative path are fairly adept at this business of self-knowledge, and when this discipline is cultivated over time, identifying thoughts is done in a flash, and one quickly returns to the prayer word or to just being in loving attentiveness before God.

Cognitive psychologists tell clients who struggle with depression to keep a catalogue of the negative thoughts that plague them. Cognitive psychology has become aware that much depression is maintained, even generated, by getting caught up in negative patterns of thinking. The more one can recognize depressive thoughts and thought patterns, the more gains are made in managing depression. Evagrius is one of a host of saints and sages with a sophisticated awareness of this very thing and how recognizing thoughts applies not simply to depression, but to a host of life issues that typically bring struggle: sexuality, security, fame, fortune, and so on. We progress in overcoming the illusion of separation from God when we learn how to deal with the barrage of thoughts that pummels us into misery. This is exactly what Evagrius is addressing.

Our normal response to an afflictive thought-feeling is to pounce on it with a commentary. In fact much of what pop psychology calls "feeling your feelings" is precisely this. When we "feel our feelings" what we feel is actually not our feelings but our *commentary* on the thought-feeling (plus whatever chemical responses take place in the body to produce sweaty palms, a knotted stomach, a racing pulse, etc.). Evagrius wants to heal this by taking it to a deeper level: meet this thought-feeling before it has a chance to grow into a dramatic story, an inner video, which, as Evagrius admits, "we run to see them."[4] Instead, simply observe the thought as it arises. Watch it come and watch it go. It's a subtle art.

This places us in a different relationship with thoughts and feelings (which, after the Second Doorway, we see are made of the same stuff). Take fear for example. What we normally watch is an elaborate array of videos about what or who frightens us, how appalling this person is, our various strategies for avoiding or manipulating him or her. Evagrius is saying don't observe the video, observe the thought-feeling before it whips itself into a video. Observe the fear or the anger or the envy—whatever the thought-feeling—and not the story we spin about the fear, the anger, the envy. It takes practice to cultivate this watchful awareness.

This watchfulness also applies to our tendency to add thought upon thought upon thought. We notice, for example, our anger and how it is quickly followed by another thought that judges it: "I should not be having this angry thought" or "after all these years I still can't let go of my anger" or "I thought I dealt with this years ago." This aggregate of thoughts must also be observed, and we must each see for ourselves that part of the reason we can't let go is that we whip these thoughts and feelings into a great drama that we watch over and over again.

It is not a question of having only acceptable thoughts, but of thoughts thoroughly observed as they appear and disappear in awareness. No thought or feeling should appear in the valley of awareness unobserved. Evagrius says to note their intensity and decline. Are the thoughts burdensome or not? Do they start out with intensity and then taper off? Are you vulnerable to certain afflictive thoughts at certain times of the day? Is it new pain or old pain with new clothes? Do thoughts arise in certain situations or with certain people? What thoughts set off a commentary? A single thought or a collision of thought upon thought upon thought? Where do they register in the body? It's really not a question of looking for information but of cultivating a contemplative discipline called watchfulness or vigilance (unknowingly rediscovered by modern cognitive psychology) that will eventually give way to meeting thoughts and feelings directly, instead of meeting them with a commentary or even with these questions just posed.

It is precisely this deeply ingrained habit of meeting thoughts with commentary, sometimes frenzied and obsessive commentary, that creates the noise in our heads, a good deal of suffering, as well as the sense of being separate from God and isolated from others. Sometimes these thoughts arrange themselves in such a way that they become a mental strategy. Among these mind games, and there are many, three are especially common: judging the quality of our own prayer, attempting to recreate positive experiences, and ego backlash.

We have a way of bringing into the uncharted land of prayer a false map of what prayer should be like. This expectation is useless, yet we nevertheless use it as the measure by which we judge our prayer. "If I am doing this correctly, my prayer ought to be this way." This judgment is simply a thought, and it is important to see it as just a thought. John Chapman writes in his *Spiritual Letters*, "One must do [this practice] for God's sake; but one will not get any satisfaction out of it in the sense of feeling 'I am good at prayer,' 'I have an infallible method.' That would be disastrous, since what we want to learn is precisely our own weakness, powerlessness, unworthiness. And one should wish for no prayer, except precisely the prayer that God gives us—probably very distracted and unsatisfactory in every way."[5] Expectations of what prayer should be like can on their own generate enough frustration to prevent passing through even the First Doorway, but they are perilous at any moment along the way. Here at the Second Doorway it is important to meet the judging thought directly, before it whips up a story about frustration or boredom. Meet it with silence. Like most distracting thoughts, it will not survive the direct meeting of a steady, silent gaze. At the very least we will come to see that it is not real in the way we previously thought it to be.

Another common knot of distractions comes after we have had what we judge to be a good period of prayer: the time flies by; there is a sense of calm recollection, even deep recollection. We then try to seize control of it in an effort to recreate it. This effort, moreover, is often coupled with the expectation that our prayer should be like this from now on. And so we pounce on it. We sit just how we were sitting at that magic moment, adjust our clothing in just the same way we did in the prayer time that went so well. Was that a shower before and a quick coffee that helped me focus? Lights dimmed just so? Scented candles? That special bell? Some of these things may help, but the point is to be able to spot the mental game we are playing with ourselves. The purpose here is not to spot the game so that we can then say to ourselves, "now stop that game playing." This is just another game. More chatter. Allow to arise whatever arises, without determining what is allowed to arise in awareness and what is not. Meet everything with a steady, silent gaze. What notices the mind game is free of the mind game.

A mountain does not determine what sort of weather is happening but witnesses all the weather that comes and goes. The weather is our thoughts, changing moods, feelings, impressions, reactions, our character plotted out for us by the Enneagram or Myers-Briggs. All of these have their place. But they are only patterns of weather. There is a deeper core that is utterly free and vast and silent, that no thought or feeling has ever entered, yet every thought and feeling appears and disappears in it. This realization that there is some deeper, silent core that grounds all our mental processes grows as we prepare to respond to these riddles of distraction with silence and not chatter, and move through the Second Doorway.

Breakthroughs do indeed happen. These can, however, be quickly followed by moodiness, irritability, struggling once again with demons we thought had been dealt with long ago. This ego backlash is fairly common at this point in one's practice and not all that complicated.[6] The ego is accustomed to keeping a tight grip on things and always having the last word. Any growth in contemplation is going to loosen the ego's grip, and the encounter with silence will for once leave it speechless. Sometimes the ego then reacts by tightening its grip again, and, after taking a step forward, we're left with the impression of having taken three steps back. It's best to become comfortable with the sense of always being a beginner. St. Gregory of Nyssa thinks it characterizes the spiritual life. In his beautiful *Homilies on the Song of Songs* Gregory points out that the Bride, no matter how much she has matured in the spiritual life "always seems to be just beginning the journey."[7] Her beginner's mind is far more spacious and conducive to contemplation than any feeling of being good at prayer.

How are we to answer the riddles of distraction that guard the Second Doorway? Like those of the First Doorway we answer them by our silence. But it is a different sort of silence. At the First Doorway we learned above all how to take refuge in the prayer word as an alternative to getting caught up in our endless dramas. With this refuge comes a certain inner silence and recollection. This silent recollection, however, is very much over and against our distractions: we're over here with our prayer word keeping at bay distractions that come at us from over there. There is nothing wrong with this silence, but the riddles of the Second Doorway are subtler and require as an answer a yet more silent and empty fullness. This is precisely what inner vigilance cultivates. As our silence deepens we are able to meet our thoughts and feelings directly, without commentary, without telling a story to ourselves about them. We simply let them be without being ensnared by them. Gradually we see the simplest of facts, so simple and yet we have missed it all these years: our thoughts and feelings appear in something deeper, in a great vastness. This vastness is not yet another object of awareness but the ground of awareness itself. Now we are close to solving the riddle.

Now that you are aware of these objects, gently shift your attention from them, these narratives that have stolen our attention over a lifetime—our anger, our fear, our envy, our pounding commentaries on how life should be—shift your attention to the awareness itself. Immediately the thinking mind grows still. Then we have answered the riddle of the Second Doorway and we realize that we are silence, fuller and vaster than the mind can grasp.

This realization is subtler than it may sound. The habits of the thinking mind are strong and have great momentum. The tendency will be to make some sort of object out of this awareness and try to visualize it as something out there. This is another mind game. You are the silent, vast awareness. Shift your attention from the mind game to the awareness itself, to the *being aware*. Here you keep silent vigil, silent awareness gazing into silent awareness.

Moving through the Second Doorway we learn something important about distractions, and really all our mental processes. Before this new threshold, distractions seemed right in our face. Our contemplative practice was a contemplative battle with distractions. But as we gradually learn to meet distractions directly, no longer needing to deflect thoughts and feelings with our prayer word, and not meeting distractions with commentary, but with a steady silent gaze, as we learn all this, the grace-filled dynamic of silence shows us how uncluttered, spacious, still, and calm our awareness is and has always been, majestic as a mountain. We learn that these distractions are no big deal: they are like weather—good weather, bad weather, boring weather—appearing before Mount Zion. Our entire discursive framework, distracting or attracting, appears in silent, vast awareness. This is a simple, clean fact known only after we have been trained by the riddles of distraction at this Second Doorway and have solved this riddle by our own inner silence. "Whoever trusts in Yahweh is like Mt. Zion: unshakeable, it stands forever" (Ps 125:1).

THE RIDDLE OF THE THIRD DOORWAY: WHAT IS THE NATURE OF THESE THOUGHTS AND FEELINGS, AND WHO IS AWARE OF THEM?

The anonymous mediaeval author of *The Cloud of Unknowing* offers helpful advice as we move through the Second Doorway toward the Third. He says, whenever you are plagued by distractions, "try to look over their shoulders, as it were, searching for something else—and that something is God, enclosed in the cloud of unknowing."[8] The author suggests a creative way to deal with distractions that involves neither getting caught up in them nor pushing them away. We have to allow distractions to be present in order to be able to look over their shoulders. But we do this in such a way as not to let them steal our attention. The television may be going, but we don't have to watch it. In this way distractions cease to be so distracting. If we let them be, we can see that they appear in something deeper: the vastness of our own awareness. This vastness is God's cloak, what the author calls the cloud of unknowing, "the dark cloud where God was" (Ex 20:21). But we must move beyond this, and this is the purpose of the riddle of the Third Doorway: to see what is the nature of thoughts and feelings and who is aware of them.

By nature I mean: Do they have any substance? Is there anything to them? Are they real in the way we think they are? In light of the fact that a significant contributing factor to our hypertension, ulcers, and fibrillation is often afflictive thoughts and feelings, these questions bear asking. Certainly something may have set them off, but as we try to sit in silent prayer, more often than not what may or may not have set them off is well in the past (if in fact it ever occurred to begin with).

Now that there is enough inner silence to see what these thoughts and feelings appear in, the whole relationship with distractions becomes different. We untangle ourselves from our afflictive thoughts much more easily. Our psychodramas no longer require three acts before they draw to conclusion. Naming thoughts has become second nature. We see very clearly the difference between a simple thought that occurs and the lengthy commentary we attach to it. There is an inner calm that even others can see and is somehow tied to an abiding empathy and respect even for those who do not wish us well. With an inner gaze that is spacious and solid, like Mount Zion that cannot be shaken, that stands forever, we can look straight into these thoughts and feelings and see that they are not real in the way we took them to be. In the beginning they seemed so real, but now we see that they cannot withstand a direct gaze. They are nothing. Empty. Look and see for yourself.

This is the great liberation of solving this third riddle, which we come to soon after the second. Inner silence is such that we meet thoughts and feelings purely and simply without commentary, the way a riverbed receives the water from up stream and lets it go down stream, all the same receptive giving. When by the grace of simple realization we see that our own depths are a luminous vastness in which our painful feelings appear, in which our judgmental thoughts appear, in which our endless mind games appear, our wounds appear, our joy, our recollection, our fear and fragmentation all appear and disappear. And yet this luminous vastness is untouched by the pain, has never been wounded, has always been pure. Pain obviously remains; anger remains; we play our mind games (probably to a lesser extent); passing joys and fleeting fears all remain. This is the human condition. But what we realize is that all these distractions are so much weather appearing on Mount Zion. When we recognize that we *are* Mount Zion, God's holy dwelling place, and no longer suffer from the illusion that we are the weather, then we are free to let life be as it is at any given moment. We are no longer the victims of our afflictive thoughts, but their vigilant witness, silent and free, no longer requiring pain to be gone if it happens to be present.

To know this is to have answered the third riddle: what is their nature? The thoughts and feelings that have brought us such delight and sorrow are also manifestations of this luminous vastness, waves of the ocean, branches of the vine. And who is aware of these distracting thoughts? Shift your attention from the distraction to the awareness itself, to the awareing. There is nothing but this same luminous vastness, this depthless depth. What gazes into luminous vastness is itself luminous vastness. There is not a separate self who is afraid or angry or jealous. Clearly fear, anger, jealousy may be present, but we won't find anyone who is afraid, angry, jealous, etc., just luminous, depthless depth gazing into luminous, depthless depth.

Now we see all this clearly, but years ago we would have taken this experience of being riven with anxiety and riveted to our inner videos as constituting who we are, and we would have grasped at joy in order to avoid pain and anguish. But now we see that this no longer holds identity, and in the face of the same anxieties and videos there is a deeper calm, a tranquility that grounds both feelings of recollection and fragmentation. Evagrius speaks of this tranquility and observes that those who know it are somehow aware of a luminous quality. Moreover, this tranquility abides even as we "behold the affairs of life."[9] Life still happens. Loved ones die; we experience tragedy, failure. Yet in all we are the tranquil awareness that grounds and presides and is one with all, whether things are going well in life or all hell is breaking loose.

Distractions—riddles of Solomon's sages—serve a purpose. If we cannot weather these distractions in stillness, they will give the impression that the doorway into the silent land is closed. But if we are simply still before them and do not try to push them away or let ourselves be carried away by them, they help deepen our contemplative practice. They initiate us into a sort of education by ordeal. The fruits of this education are manifold, but we have identified in the course of this chapter three that are fundamental.

First, we realize that we are not our thoughts and feelings. It is very liberating to realize that what goes on in our head, indeed the entire mindstream, does not have the final word on who we are. Life is simplified.

Second, once we have crossed this threshold of realizing we are not the mind-stream of thoughts and feelings, we find the tensions of life easier to live through. Our interiority is not so cramped; indeed it is a vast and spacious flow. It is as though for a lifetime we have been staring at clouds as they move across a valley, but now we see that these clouds that have obscured our vision and our very identities, to the point that we have taken them to be our very selves, exist in something deeper and vaster. Our own interiority is not a cramped space, but a valley of spaciousness. Clouds of thoughts and feelings come and go. We can identify these clouds with precision, but we no longer identify with them.

Third, we realize that what beholds this vast and flowing whole is also the whole. We see that these thoughts and feelings that have plagued us, clouded our vision, seduced us, entertained us, have no substance. They too are a manifestation of the vastness in which they appear.

I think St. Paul would simply have called this the peace of Christ, a realization of the baptismal fact of being in Christ. "I live now, not I, but Christ lives in me" (Gal 2:19–20). Christ is the way though the door and Christ is the door (Jn 10:9).

SIX

From Victim to Witness:
Practicing with Affliction

I'm an old man now and have had a great many problems.
Most of them never happened.

—*Mark Twain*

Attentiveness is the heart's stillness, unbroken by any thought.
—*Hesychios of Sinai*

The previous chapters have emphasized the dynamics involved in three important components of contemplative practice: the role of the body, working with a prayer word, and meeting distractions. This chapter will revisit some of this material but from a different perspective. We shall look at examples of how contemplative practice can contribute to, even transfigure, the struggle with afflictive emotions. There are a couple of reasons for doing this. First, it gives us the advantage of seeing what some of these struggles can look like when they have human faces. Second, when one person's experience is shared, there is something for each of us to learn, even if the details of our own struggle may differ quite a lot and are far less extreme than the ones we will consider here. The portraits we will look at in this chapter depict struggles with fear, pain, and fragmented craving. In each of these cases I have changed certain details to protect privacy.

PARALYZED BY FEAR

Why look at fear? Fear is a perfectly appropriate emotion. An unexpected noise occurs, and we are startled. We put down our Stephen King novel and start bolting all the doors and windows of the house. But for some of us fear is not always so straightforward. Indeed for many of us fear can be something insidious that can paralyze self-confidence and generate self-loathing, as it was for one particular woman.

Laura (let us call her) had lived some eight or ten years in her monastery before she was forced to meet fear. Her early years in the community weren't without problems, but she was aware that she had grown to love these women and that in this community she could give herself completely to God. One day a life-changing event occurred. She had a run-in with another nun in the community. There was a public disagreement between the two over how a general community policy should best be implemented in a particular situation. It became a rather one-sided verbal punch-up. Laura knew that she had always been petrified of "that woman" (as the nun was henceforth termed), but from the time of this disagreement, fear began to govern her life. Fear jumped behind the wheel of the car.

One of the advantages of living in a well-ordered community like a monastery is that you can account for nearly everybody's whereabouts at any given time. Laura knew down which stairs and at what time that woman would descend for chapel, around which corner and down which corridor that woman would come to meals. Laura could avoid her easily. The community had the custom of processing two-by-two into chapel for prayers. She learned how, with a change of pace and a deferential bow, she could avoid pairing up with that woman.

The community had a particular rule that said, "let no one draw you out of quiet recollection." It was a simple rule meant to serve something important: environmental silence that supports the life of prayer and attentiveness. This too she could conscript into the service of avoidance and refusal to speak to that woman. Notice what Laura did: silence as a context for seeking God was co-opted into silence as avoidance, the cold silence of the cold shoulder. She learned to manage fear by avoiding that woman. This went on for a couple of years.

This strategy of managing fear is understandable enough. She felt threatened and so protected herself. What Laura did not know, however, was that this subtle way of indulging fear actually makes it grow; telling ourselves a story about the fear and then acting out this story, increases the momentum of fear. It strengthens fear's grip.

Her fear grew like bindweed. Avoiding that woman was not the only way that fear began to take charge of her life. It took over everything. She began to fear that the community was going get rid of her and leave her penniless. She began to fear that the community was going to disband and that she would be homeless. She began to fear that when it rained it was never going to stop raining and she would drown. When she refused one day to come out from under her bed, the superior of the community thought some counseling might be in order.

TURNING THE TABLES ON FEAR

Learning to confront fear, indeed any afflictive emotion, is one of the great spiritual arts; it is liberating and energizing. Barry Lopez gives a powerful account of this in *Arctic Dreams*, where he describes the role of the polar bear among the Eskimos. For the Eskimos the polar bear is a deadly enemy, and humans are sometimes easy prey. Yet the polar bear is an important source of food and clothing and plays a significant role in the Eskimos' religious and cultural life. To confront the polar bear was a right of passage that brought a new sense of inner strength.

The Eskimo word for polar bear is *Tornarrsuk*, meaning "the one who gives power." "To encounter the bear," Lopez continues, "to meet it with your whole life, was to grapple with something personal. The confrontation occurred on a serene, deadly, and elevated plain. If you were successful you found something irreducible within yourself. To walk away was to be alive, utterly. To be assured of your own life, the life of your kind, in a harsh land where life took insight and patience and humor. It was to touch the bear. It was a gift from the bear."[1] Confronting fear bestows a gift.

The therapist taught Laura some basic skills in confrontation: not how to confront that woman, not how to confront the situations that frightened her, but how to confront *fear itself*, how to receive the "gift from the bear."

Laura made steady progress. Before she started dealing with fear she felt completely caught up in fear; either victimized by it or acting out of it. With the help of her therapist, she learned how to distinguish between the object of fear, that woman, and the fear itself. The therapist hoped Laura would learn that there was more to herself than the fear, that there was something within her that was not afraid. This may seem obvious to the point of being ridiculous, but it was not at all obvious to Laura. The therapist had Laura give a name to this fear. She named it "Frances."

The practice was for Laura to keep a sharp eye on Frances. And whenever Frances pushed Laura to one side and got behind the wheel of the car, Laura would tell Frances to return to the passenger side. In her journal she would keep track of what Frances had been up to that day. Thus she learned gradually to distinguish herself from fear and not to be so afraid of fear. She became so dedicated to confronting fear in this way that she would wait for that woman to turn up just so she could practice distinguishing the experience of fear from the object of fear, distinguishing Frances from that woman.

This simple practice that Laura learned is an ancient contemplative practice called vigilance or watchfulness. Remember Evagrius's instruction: "Let him keep careful watch over his thoughts. Let him observe their intensity, their periods of decline and follow them as they rise and fall."[2] Evagrius doesn't say to give these afflictive thoughts a human name like "Frances," but he does counsel naming the afflictive thought in the sense of identifying it as anger, envy, pride, etc.[3] The fruit of this practice is that we disentangle ourselves from the afflictive emotion without denying it, without repressing it, without acting out.

Laura gradually disentangled herself from the bramble of fear. The bramble was there, but increasingly she stayed out of the bramble. The sessions tapered off and eventually came to an end. But this was not the end of the journey.

To meet this God "in whom we live and move and have our being" (Acts 17:28) there must be a yet deeper liberation. This is where most psychotherapeutic strategies of managing afflictive emotions such as fear leave off, but where the contemplative disciplines continue.

In the midst of this struggle with fear Laura had experienced a renewed dedication to contemplative practice. The Jesus Prayer united to her breath took root in her heart, and here she made her home. She found great support in a line by

Hesychios, which she kept in her prayer book, on her desk, and at her work place: "Attentiveness is the heart's stillness, unbroken by any thought. In this stillness the heart breathes and invokes, endlessly and without ceasing, only Jesus Christ who is the Son of God and Himself God."[4] Moreover, she found that this practice worked well with her other practice of keeping an eye on the whereabouts of Frances.

Hesychios sees these practices as complementary forms of watchfulness. "One type of watchfulness consists in closely scrutinizing every mental image or provocation."[5] This is basically the skill that the therapist taught Laura. This watchfulness is not our superego's monitor, ever ready to shame us into conformity to an internalized ideal of what holiness is supposed to look like. Watchfulness is a contemplative practice that awakens and refines the silent witness within each of us. It is free of all ego strategies that hold onto what we like or push away what we don't like. It is a grounding, vigilant receptivity. This witness, that which is *aware* of the afflictive emotion, that which is *aware* of clinging to it or fleeing from it, is itself free of the affliction, free of the clinging, free of the fleeing.

Hesychios goes on to identify another type of watchfulness, the direction in which Laura was moving. "A second type of watchfulness consists in freeing the heart from all thoughts, keeping it profoundly silent and still, and in praying. A third type consists in continually and humbly calling upon the Lord Jesus Christ for help."[6] For Hesychios, watchfulness includes awareness of thoughts, being their witness and not their victim, as well as working with the prayer word. It is likely that Hesychios had in mind the Jesus Prayer as the third type of watchfulness. It is precisely the practice of the Jesus Prayer (or any fruitful working with a prayer word) that helps keep the heart "profoundly silent and still." This is the gift Laura was receiving. Her practice of the Jesus Prayer was revealing a deeper silence, a silence that did not require fear to be gone. It led to a breakthrough that Laura did not expect: *fear itself becomes a vehicle of deeper silence.*

With the help of her therapist Laura had learned how to distinguish the objects of fear from the fear itself. But through her own contemplative practice she learned something else. The inner stability and stillness, which result from a well-established practice, allowed Laura not only to distinguish the objects of fear from the fear itself, but also *to be still* in the midst of fear. This is not the stillness of a rabbit hiding from a predator, but the stillness of a mountain presiding over a valley. She was learning not to react to the presence of fear; she could simply meet fear with stillness instead of meeting it with her reactive commentary on fear. Fear was present, but she was not afraid of fear. This transformed her relationship with fear.

The presence of fear was no longer experienced as a threat but as an opportunity to practice being "profoundly still and silent, and praying," as Hesychios puts it. Her experience of fear had changed from fear as mind-tripping panic to fear as vehicle of silence. It had changed from seeing fear as an enemy to be conquered to seeing fear as a tool for deepening. Through her practice of the Jesus Prayer, fear was transformed from obstacle to aid.

But this is not the end of the story. A new crisis presented itself. She was told that she might be asked to move to a different house of her Order. The following day her mother died of stroke, and by the end of the week, her father had died of heart attack. This threw her into a panic that stayed with her for some weeks. She said she felt as though the panic had grabbed her and was shaking her senseless. She felt she would break.

However, she did not break; nor did she resort to hiding under her bed. Even in the midst of the rattling panic she could manage times during her ordinary daily tasks to practice the Jesus Prayer united with her breath, so that even during these activities she could simply be "profoundly still and silent, and praying." This was a tremendous step forward. But she could see that even here there was something self-centered. It was a subtle ego-strategy whose goal was to get rid of fear: if she could be silent in the midst of fear, then fear would go away.

Then something happened in her practice that had never happened before. Some welling up of grace prompted her to look straight into the fear. She did not react to the fear; she did not fear the fear; she did not demand that the fear be gone. She saw this fear for what it was: a mass of thoughts and feelings and an unpleasant tension in the body. That's all fear was. It wasn't real in the way she had thought; it had no firmness, no shape. What gave fear its power was the story going on in her head about the fear and the belief that she was this story of fear. Fear was present. It registered in her gut. But she was not the fear.

She was still aware of fear, but what was aware of the fear was free of fear. This awareness, herself aware, simply aware, no demands, no strategies, was infinitely vaster than the fear. Her life of struggle with fear was not separate from life as Presence of God. These two are as one.

NOT AFRAID OF FEAR

Laura's transforming encounter with fear reveals not the disappearance of fear but the disappearance of struggling with fear. Fear remains present, but she is not afraid of fear. The struggle with any afflictive thought or feeling is the result of the noisy chatter of the mind. This chattering, commenting mind turns the simple experience of any thought or feeling into an experience of grasping or fleeing. When this mental chatter is brought to stillness, the struggle relaxes and the nature of fear is seen to be different from what we previously thought. As Eckhart put it, "what was previously an obstacle to you is now a great help."[7] Fear as affliction is transformed into fear as vehicle of Presence.

The key is to move from being a victim of thoughts (the commenting, chattering mind) to being their witness (the heart's stillness). Thoughts and feelings remain, but this move from victim to witness transforms our relationship with affliction. Laura's struggle with fear ultimately revealed this gradual transformation that took place over several stages. Though there were backward and sideward movements, as well as stretches of no movement, we can see three key moments, doorways if you will, in her transformation from victim to witness.

1. Caught in the Grip of Reaction

If you want to make fear grow, run from it. Create strategies to avoid meeting it directly. Hide it under outbursts of rage or blame; no one will dare look for it there. This is precisely what Laura did.

A large part of the struggle with fear is actually an inability to experience fear directly. Laura really never met fear directly and simply. She didn't actually "feel her feelings," though she used the threadbare phrase. She was afraid, indeed petrified, but what she was "feeling" was the reaction to her wild commentary on fear. She was completely caught up in the story she was telling herself about fear, about that woman, which then became a story about abandonment, and ultimately, grew out of all control and proportion.

Fear pushed her up and down the corridors of her life and then right under her bed. The complete identification with the story going on in our heads about fear distorts self-knowledge and increases the obsessive thinking that makes us prisoners. Teresa of Avila speaks pointedly about obsessing on fear and its effects. "These fears arise from not knowing ourselves. Fear distorts knowledge of self. What we really should be afraid of is obsessing over ourselves and never getting free of ourselves!"[8] Distorted self-knowledge is the result of anxious commentary on fear, panic, and dread. Any sense that, as Teresa puts it, "the sun is shining at her center" was not available to her.[9]

2. Stability in the Midst of Fear

Laura eventually discovered an inner stability even in the midst of fear. Crossing this threshold, Laura learned to distinguish the fear itself from the object of fear (that woman). Gradually she learned to see that there was a difference between fear as a simple emotion and the mind's lightning-quick commentary on fear.

This skill of observation and discernment, which the ancients call "vigilance," has three elements. First, turn around and meet the afflictive emotion with stillness. Without a dedicated practice this won't be possible. Second, allow fear to be present. Third, let go of the commentary on the fear. This third element is the most challenging.

It is often difficult to let go of the story, in spite of our willingness to do so. The difficulty is due to the momentum generated by mental habits of watching our internal videos, listening to our mental chatter decade after decade. This is precisely where our contemplative practice offers practical assistance.

Whenever we become aware of either watching another video about the fear or trying to push the fear away, we simply return to our practice. It is not a question of controlling whether or not the attention will be stolen (it will be); it is a question of returning to our practice when we become aware that the attention has been stolen. This gradually cultivates inner stillness and creates a new mental habit of not indulging the story, but instead simply letting the story be there if it happens to be there. With time the story will be less victimizing and may even play itself out.

Over time the chatter loses its grip, and we feel more stable even in the midst of chaos. Hesychios says this "inner stability produces a natural intensification of watchfulness; and this intensification gradually and in due measure gives contemplative insight into spiritual warfare. This in turn is succeeded by persistence in the Jesus Prayer and by the state that Jesus confers, in which the mind, free of all images, enjoys complete silence."[10] Heyschios is describing the basic dynamic of contemplative practice that frees us and helps us move from victim to witness. Growth in inner stability, even in the midst of chaos, deepens our capacity to be aware of what is happening within us *as it is happening*. With this move from passive victim to vigilant witness we begin to see with greater clarity the fits of obsessive commentary that we supply.

Hesychios refers to this as "insight into spiritual warfare." At times it is an ordeal, but the result is that we can delve more deeply into the prayer and the silence it bestows. Thus, more grounded in our practice, we face inner chaos with greater stability. This inner stability helps us detach from the mental chatter; thereby we are led into deeper silence.

In this dynamic process of inner silencing, our afflictive thoughts and feelings are seen in a new light. Now we can see how afflictive thoughts and feelings play a rather important role. They provide an invitation to be still and gaze into the silent vastness they manifest. This is how Eckhart could say, "what used to be a hindrance now helps you most." Such is the simple sifting of silence.

3. Seeing through Fear

If you want to know the true nature of fear, look straight into it. Fear, anger, envy—any afflictive thought or feeling—cannot withstand a direct gaze. But if we look at the *story* and feed on the story we tell ourselves of our fear, anger, envy, etc., affliction thrives. Affliction feeds off the noise of the commenting, chattering mind.

Laura's practice of vigilance and inner silence led her to see this for herself. Moreover, she could see that there were strategies of control embedded even in contemplative practice: if I can just go deeply enough into silence, there will be no more fear in my life. By looking directly into the fear before the mind adds a story we see that fear is not real in the way we thought it was. It is nothing more than "a mass of thoughts and feelings and an unpleasant tension in the body."

What we have observed of fear can be observed of practically any struggle with afflictive thoughts and feelings. We must move from being a victim of these thoughts to being their witness. Typically we spend many, many years being their victim. We are imprisoned by the chattering mind. Gradually we learn to distinguish the simple thought or emotion from the chatter and we discover an inner stability that grows into the silence of God.

PAIN AND THE BEAUTY OF IRISES

Elizabeth was one of the world's authorities on irises. As an academic botanist she knew everything there was to know about rhizomes. When she wasn't in her lab—a large greenhouse that took up most of her back garden—she was writing up her research or attending conferences. But the onset of a rare, autoimmune disease brought all her activity to an abrupt halt. The illness left her with intense pain and bedridden much of the time. Medication had little effect. Most days she could manage but a short walk in her garden and greenhouse to inspect the irises.

Elizabeth's pain was simply there. But her active mind could not let the pain be. Her mind would pick at it, lance it, scratch at it: "Why did this have to happen?" "Who is going to take care of me?" "How can I pay for this?" There were times of the day when the pain would intensify, and her thoughts ran: "Wouldn't it be better to die," "I don't want to be a burden to others," or "Why is God punishing me?" When the thoughts let up, she would soon be looking at the clock in anticipation of the next battle. "My thoughts are like a pack of hyenas. They make the pain unbearable."

Elizabeth was familiar with contemplative practice but said it had been "more or less limited to airports, train journeys and enduring tedious sermons." With the onset of this illness, however, her spiritual well-being became more of a concern to her, and so she established a regular discipline spaced through each day. There was no question of Elizabeth using any of the traditional prayer postures discussed earlier. She could only lie on her back in bed. But out of this renewed dedication to the practice of contemplation she learned a lot about coping with pain. Giving her attention to her prayer word and her breath instead of her torturing thoughts kept her in the present moment and gradually helped her distinguish the pain from the commentary on the pain.

Her rediscovery of prayer bore fruit not only in a deepened awareness of God's abiding presence, but also she became skilled at seeing how the drama of the commenting mind adds to suffering. As a result she discovered several important things about pain.

Thoughts about pain are worse than pain by itself. "Suffering is what your mind does with your pain," she said. "A silent mind knows no suffering." Trying to push pain away increases suffering. In her case there was no question of pain going away. But suffering she could do something about. If she could be still before the pain and not wrestle with it, she felt alive and aware. Gradually she was able to let go of the demand that the pain be gone, if it didn't happen to be gone.

By learning simply to be still before pain she learned to see into pain. Pain has a center. This center is silence. When her attention was not stolen by thoughts about the pain, she could be still before this silent center. In this silent center she felt closest to God, so she would go back there whenever she could. It was not long after this discovery that she had the breakthrough of her life.

A quiet mind enabled her to see that silence is not separate from pain. Certainly silence is not pain, but neither is the pain separate from the silence. However, if she got lost in *thoughts about the pain*, then she returned to suffering. But what brought definitive change for the remaining time before her death was the realization that in this very silence there was communion with all people, a loving solidarity with *all humanity*. The awareness of this was seamlessly united with her awareness of God. This realization expressed itself—even while bedridden—as self-forgetful, loving attentiveness to all whom she met.

Health-care professionals, family, and friends arrived to help her and left feeling helped by her. They would end up bringing up their own problems, their own life pain. She would say, "Don't *think* about the pain. *Be still* before the pain." She didn't mean to give, and they didn't intend to receive. But the more she was able to surrender to the loving silence at the center of her pain, the more she was a vehicle of this loving silence.

Medical writer Steven Levine observes "true healing happens when we go into our pain so deeply that we see it, not just as our pain, but everyone's pain. It is immensely moving and supportive to discover that my pain is not private to me." This is precisely what Elizabeth discovered about pain. If she could be silent within herself, in the midst of her pain, and not get caught up in commenting on the pain, she saw her isolation vanish and what she found, even in the midst of this pain, was communion with all people in the silence of God.

Elizabeth moved from being a *victim* of suffering to being a *witness* of pain by letting go of the demand that the pain be other than it happens to be at any given moment. She hurt. But she did not suffer. Once we know that in silence is our self, we know that the dimensionless depth within it does not cling to or push away anything. What we once saw as an obstacle or something that isolated us from God, ourselves, others, is now a place of communion. This subtle transformation is beautifully expressed by Simone Weil. "Two prisoners whose cells adjoin communicate with each other by knocking on the wall. The wall is the thing which separates them but is also their means of communication. It is the same with us and God. Every separation is a link."[11]

The key to opening the doorway of this discovery—that "every separation is a link"—is silence. Whether we are dealing with physical pain or emotional pain, be still before this pain until you see its silent center that contains the whole universe. "Be still and know that I am God" (Ps 46:10).

Not long before Elizabeth died she was talking about how she missed her life as a botanist, about the unfinished projects that would remain unfinished. She said, "You know, while I've been ill I have managed to discover something new about irises—I never knew they were beautiful."

THE CHAOS OF CRAVING

James is a recovering addict. Like many before him he became addicted to crack after his first use. "I took the crack, then the crack took me." He finally hit bottom with such a thud that he was too stunned to resist the help at the treatment center he went to. Then he moved to a halfway house.

Next door to this halfway house is a convent of sisters. They have taught him how to sit still and how to be in silence. He feels safe in their chapel. The space is nourishing and calming. He goes there nearly every morning before work to sit in silence and to share in their community prayer.

The treatment facility considers James one of its success stories. James, however, does not see himself as a success story. He thinks success means no more struggle and he still struggles intensely. People who know him, however, see a man of reverential calm and deep compassion.

James has had only one slip in five years. But on any given day there could be a near miss. He looks and acts perfectly normal. "People look at me and presume that because I appear to be reasonably well put together, everything is fine. They have no idea what it is like for me on the inside, how each day is an ordeal just coping with the storms of chaos in my mind." James attributes what others call success to two things he's learned: how to reach within in order to reach out. He has a solid network of support that helps him reach out to others, and his contemplative practice is his lifeline.

"I can be feeling fine and then I'll walk past a flower stand and begin to convulse with this inner chaos and I'll want to use." The street his dealer lived on had a flower stand on the corner. James has never returned to that part of town where his dealer lived, but a flower stand, any flower stand, still has a powerful enough hold on his memory that it arouses the frenzied, fragmented craving that drags him to the edge.

As Evagrius observed long ago, "the memory has a powerful proclivity for causing detriment to the spirit."[12] James feels most vulnerable when he is under pressure to be productive or has too much time on his hands or when he is upset or lacking self-confidence—in other words, when trying to get through a normal day.

"The problem with my head is that it's not content with peace of mind. I can be having a wonderful day, and then out of the blue something in me begins the pre-use ritual. I'll start checking to see if I want to use. If I don't want to use, my mind often won't be content with that. It will try to scratch the itch to make it itch so that I can then scratch it. My heart begins to pound and my stomach tightens and shudders. This fragmented craving will be moving in several directions at once. There's the memory of the thrilling rush. There's my present awareness that, since I've stopped using, the so-called rush never was so thrilling but more of a muzzle over my pain and anxiety. And there's the seductive voice of the future that says, 'Yes, but this time it will work. It'll be wonderful. You can control it. No one will know.' All these are colliding in my head."

James's struggle with this demon doesn't differ much from Evagrius's description of the demon stirring up "thoughts of various affairs by means of the memory. He [the demon] stirs up all the passions.... In this way he hopes to offer some obstacle to that excellent course pursued in prayer on the journey toward God."[13] James's practice of contemplation made a real contribution to how he experienced his struggles.

Until James learned about contemplative practice, God wasn't really part of his life. But this way of being still, of *just being*, awakened in him a longing for truth and a sense of loving presence within. "The payoff was the calming of my inner turmoil. There is something within me that the turmoil doesn't reach. And I cling to my breath and my prayer word like a dog to a bone. I need to know this space where all is calm. I've heard about the great saints going through periods of darkness and a sense of abandonment by God. I really couldn't cope with that in my present state. I need this God who draws me to silence."

The more he gave himself to his practice, the more skilled he became at observing the workings of his mind. He could spot the pre-use ritual—the mind trying to scratch an itch—and could see the powerful momentum of compulsive mental habits. He could also see that this momentum needed two things: inner chaos and a state of isolation produced by the chaos. If he interrupted this dynamic early enough and returned to his prayer word and his breath, instead of getting caught in the inner chaos, then the mental storm would not develop. But when the inner noise produced the state of isolation, the prayer word wasn't enough.

Frenzy feeds on isolation. He knows he needs to distract himself by throwing himself into work or establishing contact with people in order to stop the spiraling of isolation. Teresa of Avila came to a similar realization of how best to cope with severe trials. Speaking of a slightly different situation she counseled, "Although there is no cure for such a malady, the best medicine for achieving temporary relief is to engage in external work and service and to hope in the mercy of God who never fails those who hope in him."[14]

"Usually if I talk to someone, the chaos will fizzle out and I'll calm down. The crucial thing is to pick up the phone. I'll get out my phone, then put it away, then get it out again and finally ring someone. Sometimes I just begin to talk to the person selling the flowers." The key is to reach out. The more he does this the easier it becomes. Human contact unties the strait jacket of inner isolation.

"Prayer has shown me the calm at the center of the storm, something that is silent even when the chaos rages." Once during a particularly difficult storm of inner chaos something happened that he could only call a spiritual breakthrough. "One morning I was sitting in the chapel where I like to go to pray. The chaos was pretty bad. I thought my head was going to explode. I can't really describe what happened next, but it was as though while trying to pray I fell into hell. I stopped fighting and just prayed there in hell. Then I felt a welling up of love within me, a love for all people who struggle, who screw up, who have been defined out of the picture, people who despair, people who are told they aren't the right race, gender or orientation. I saw how I was part of all this, how I judge people who fail and condemn people who are different. I saw how it was all tied to my self-loathing. And there I prayed in solidarity with all people who struggle. I moved beyond my self-loathing and felt one with all these people." This insight may explain why people see in him such a reverential calm and respect for others.

It is important to see what James was freed from. For a moment he was free from the self-loathing that manifests itself as condemnation of others. And in this precious moment he glimpsed the ground of love that binds us all together. Through his own journey of prayer, struggle, vulnerability, and community, he has glimpsed, however briefly, that precious gateway into the silent land.

His struggles have not gone away, but he struggles less with his struggle. And when he sits in prayer, he sits in interceding solidarity with all who don't pray, all who struggle and fail, all whom society marginalizes. Just consenting to be *still* in the midst of inner fragmentation has become an act of solidarity, a way of interceding for and being in solidarity with all people who struggle and feel as though they fail in this struggle most of the time. His struggle with inner chaos and fragmentation is becoming a real anchor.

Here were three portraits of struggle—fear, pain, compulsion—but they could depict any struggle. To the noisy mind these are all obstacles to God. But to the mind that has become silent these obstacles are vehicles of the silence of God. Eckhart reminds us again, "In fact, what used to be a hindrance now

helps you most. . . . For in all things you notice only God."[15]
As Simone Weil expresses it, "Every separation is a link."[16]

One of the great paradoxes of the spiritual life is that our struggles are not separate from the luminous vastness within each of us. We don't get rid of struggle to discover this open space; nor does its discovery necessarily rid us of our struggles. The riddle of the obstacle is solved not by pushing it away or by holding on to it, but by meeting it with silence and by discovering in this meeting that sacred ground, which upholds both joy and sorrow, both struggle and freedom from struggle. When we realize this we will struggle less with our struggles and we will have solved by our own silence the riddles that guard the doorway into the silent land.

Most of us live much of our lives caught in the whirlwind of the stories going on in our heads. As our contemplative practice matures we are presented with opportunities to drop the story and to look straight into these thoughts and feelings that lead many of us around by a nose ring. And we see they are without substance. Without the story, they have no power. This insight is behind Mark Twain's famous line. "I'm an old man now and have had a great many problems. Most of them never happened." A lot goes on in our heads that is quite worthless. The silent mind knows that what sees the fear, the pain, the inner chaos, is free of the fear, pain, or chaos. But for the noisy mind it all becomes a huge problem.

Contemplation is the way out of the great self-centered psychodrama. When interior silence is discovered, compassion flows. If we deepen our inner silence, our compassion for others is deepened. We cannot pass through the doorways of silence without becoming part of God's embrace of all humanity in its suffering and joy.

Silence is living, dynamic, and liberating. The practice of silence nourishes vigilance, self-knowledge, letting go, and the compassionate embrace of all whom we would otherwise be quick to condemn. Gradually we realize that whatever it is in us that sees the mind games we play is itself free of all such mind games and is utterly silent, pure, vast, and free. When we realize we are the *awareness* and not the drama unfolding in our awareness our lives are freer, simpler, more compassionate. Fear remains frightening but *we* are not afraid of fear. Pain still hurts, but *we* are not hurt by pain.

SEVEN

The Liturgy of Our Wounds:
Temptation, Humility, and Failure

Through his wounds we are healed.

—*Isaiah 53:5*

About this thorn in the flesh, I have pleaded with the Lord
three times for it to leave me.

—*2 Corinthians 12:8*

Life is fits and starts, mostly fits.
—*Walker Percy,* The Thanatos Syndrome

The doorway into the silent land is a wound. Silence lays
bare this wound. We do not journey far along the spiritual
path before we get some sense of the wound of the human
condition, and this is precisely why not a few abandon a contemplative practice like meditation as soon as it begins to ex-
pose this wound; they move on instead to some spiritual
entertainment that will maintain distraction. Perhaps this is
why the weak and wounded, who know very well the vulnerability of the human condition, often have an aptitude for discovering silence and can sense the wholeness and healing that
ground this wound.

There is something seductive about the contemplative path.
"I am going to seduce her and lead her into the desert and

speak to her heart" (Hosea 2:14), says Yahweh to Israel. It is tempting to think it is a superior path. More often, however, the seduction is to think we can use our practice of contemplation as a way to avoid facing our woundedness: if we can just go deeply enough into contemplation, we won't struggle any longer. It is common enough to find people taking a cosmetic view of contemplation, and then, after considerable time and dedication to contemplative practice, discover that they still have the same old warts and struggles they hoped contemplation would remove or hide. They think that somewhere they must have gone wrong.

Certainly there is deep conversion, healing, and unspeakable wholeness to be discovered along the contemplative path. The paradox, however, is that this healing is revealed when we discover that our wound and the wound of God are one wound. The poet Geoffrey Hill explores this with searing economy in the final section of "The Pentecost Castle":

> I shall go down
> to the lovers' well
> and wash this wound
> that will not heal
>
> beloved soul
> what shall you see
> nothing at all
> yet eye to eye
>
> depths of non-being
> perhaps too clear
> my desire dying
> as I desire.[1]

Silence lays bare this wound that seems to be with us for life and brings us face to face, "eye to eye" with what feels like nothing at all. In this spaciousness we wash in "the lovers' well" and discover that what may strike the senses as nothing at all, is paradoxically an overflowing fullness, what Geoffrey Hill calls "an emptiness ever thronging."[2] Silence alone will lead us to this discovery.

However, this discovery often does not feel as much like a breakthrough as it feels like breakdown. This is actually a very important and creative period in the development of our practice, but it feels as though our life is coming unpinned, that we're losing it, that we are going round the bend. Mary Richards has captured this creative chaos well. "Symptoms of growth may look like breakdown or derangement; the more we are allowed by the love of others and by self-understanding to live through our derangement into the new arrangement, the luckier we are. It is unfortunate when our anxiety over what looks like personal confusion or dereliction blinds us to the forces of liberation at work."[3] This is why for Christians the joyful faith in the Risen One never loses sight of the Crucified One.

God in Christ has taken into Himself the brokenness of the human condition. Hence, human woundedness, brokenness, death itself are transformed from dead ends to doorways into Life. In the divinizing humanity of Christ, bruises become balm. "Yet ours were the sufferings he was bearing, ours the sorrows he was carrying … and we have been healed by his bruises" (Is 53:4–5).

Some of the Christian churches perform the meaning of this transformation in a simple yet profound way at the Easter

Vigil. In the Roman Catholic liturgy, for example, the Easter candle is brought forward after the blessing of the Easter fire. A cross is then etched in the wax with a stylus, and five grains of fragrant incense are inserted in this cross—top, bottom, left, right, and center—at the five places where Christ was wounded (head, feet, each hand, and side). Meanwhile this prayer is said, "By his holy and glorious wounds may Christ our Lord guard us and keep us." Through these wounds of incense this theology in wax has something very important to say about our own wounds. Because of the death and resurrection of Jesus, wounds, failure, disgrace, death itself all have a hidden potential for revealing our deepest ground in God. Our wounds bear the perfumed trace of divine presence.

There is a deeply ingrained tendency, however, to recoil from our own brokenness, to judge it as others have judged it, to loathe it as we have been taught over a lifetime to loathe it. In doing this we avoid what God in Christ draws close to and embraces. Thomas Merton expresses this movingly. "The Christ we find in ourselves is not identified with what we vainly seek to admire and idolize in ourselves—on the contrary, he has identified himself with what we resent in ourselves, for he has taken upon himself our wretchedness and our misery, our poverty and our sins.... We will never find peace if we listen to the voice of our own fatuous self-deception that tells us the conflict has ceased to exist. We will find peace when we can listen to the 'death dance' in our blood, not only with equanimity but with exultation because we hear within it the echoes of the victory of the Risen Savior."[4] God meets the human condition where it stands most in need, in its poverty and brokenness, and as we make our pilgrim way along the path of contemplation, we will certainly meet, as Merton puts it, "what we resent most in ourselves."

St. Paul knew what it was to be wounded. He talked of his "thorn in the flesh." He had the good sense not to tell anyone what it was, but whatever sort of issue afflicted him, he seemed to struggle with it for quite some time. We can hear his frustration. "About this, I have three times pleaded with the Lord that it might leave me, but he has answered me, 'My grace is enough for you: for power is at full stretch in weakness'" (2 Cor 12:8–9). What Paul wanted was relief from his struggle. What he received instead was God.

He doesn't say how long it took him to realize that this struggle, this wound, became a vehicle of some deeper strength, but he comes out with his famous insight. "It is, then, about my weaknesses that I am happiest of all to boast, so that the power of Christ may rest upon me; and that is why I am glad of weaknesses. . . . For it is when I am weak that I am strong" (2 Cor 12:9–10).

This is precisely where contemplative practice places us: where the balm of divinity anoints broken humanity. The indwelling presence of Christ, the fragrant grains of wounded incense, makes our poverty rich and our brokenness whole.

The practice of contemplation teaches us how *to be* in this wound. When we discover the silent core of this wound, we discover a place of noncondemnation, of silent, loving communion with God and of compassion for all. In what follows I would like to explore two areas where we commonly meet our wounds: temptation and failure. Our wounds don't strike us as anything but brokenness and failure. But when we enter the silence that is the ground of all, what we make of our brokenness and failure gradually comes to look very different.

THE BENEFIT OF TEMPTATION

One of the more sobering realizations along the contemplative path is that no matter how many breakthroughs we might make, we continue to struggle to a greater or lesser degree with the same old baggage, temptations, and failings that we have always struggled with. St. Teresa of Avila observes that those who have not journeyed very far along the contemplative path "might think that the souls who have received these special favors must be so secure that they have nothing to lament—no fears, no imperfections—and can just relax now into enjoying the Beloved forever."[5] But as she knows, nothing could be further from the truth. The issues may vary in intensity, frequency, or nature, but struggle, and, alas, transgression, there will always be. The cloak of humility that unfolds into divine awareness is cut from the cloth of this struggle, and the fabric of failure is itself woven from the threads of sin and grace. What does change, however, is *how* we meet temptation. As our practice matures and deepens it gradually dawns on us what role temptation has in our contemplative training and how important it is to know how to use it wisely.

Eckhart says something startlingly sensible about temptation. "The impulse to sin always brings great benefit for someone who is righteous."[6] By "righteous" Eckhart does not mean a moral know-it-all, but a flowering of personal integrity that is characterized by ever-deepening immersion in God and in self-forgetful service to others. Hence, Eckhart is clearly addressing people who have a serious and mature commitment to the spiritual path.

There is nothing especially subtle in what Eckhart is saying. To make his point a bit more obvious he contrasts two types of righteous people. One "is the type of person who experiences little or no temptation while the other is the type who is much troubled by temptation."[7] Those who struggle with temptation are clearly the more impressive. For even though they struggle to resist sin, at the same time they remain fixed on God. "These are far worthier of praise and deserving of a far greater reward, and are far nobler than the first type, for the perfection of virtue is born in struggle, as St. Paul says, 'virtue is perfected in struggle'" (2 Cor 12:9).[8] Trial, temptation, and struggle are the making of the contemplative. Take away these and you take away tremendous opportunity for growth, depth, and wisdom.

Christian contemplatives of the early centuries observed that in the midst of Jesus' temptation in the desert he refrained from entering into dialogue with Satan. Instead of getting caught up in noisy commentary on the thoughts Satan was placing in his head, Jesus quoted lines of Scripture. Down the centuries this practice gradually becomes the Christian prayer word. Hence, the Christian contemplative tradition sees an explicit connection between the practice of prayer and confronting temptation. Just as we saw that there was more to the use of a prayer word than merely shielding oneself from distractions, so there is more to meeting temptation than simply warding it off.

The value of temptation is not really seen until our practice begins to deepen. Before we have begun to cultivate inner silence, our experience of temptation is going to be like facing a strong headwind, and we are more likely to be blown off course. With some perseverance in our practice, however, we will begin to get a sense of the opportunity for deepening what is latent in our struggles. At some point we will be able to let go of our usual victimizing-victim relationship with temptation and simply be still before it. Far from being a sort of passive resignation, this requires a deeply engaged and vigilant receptivity. Simply allow temptation to be in your awareness, without commenting on it, without dramatizing it, without generating a video about it. Simply meet it with stillness. To do this is to relate to temptation in a new way. Let's consider an example.

A temptation many of us struggle with is the temptation to judge others. Few transgressions are more strongly condemned in the New Testament. "Do not judge and you will not be judged" (Mt 7:1). Yet we are caught up in it before we know it. Moreover, it is not always easy to see what is so wrong about judging people; surely it is a basic life skill to be able to assess people and situations. But even with the most halting of footsteps in the silent land, we see that judging others really is not about our perceptions and assessments of others, but the way in which the jaws of our convictions lock so tightly around people that we actually think we know what life is like for them, what they really ought to do or think, as though we know their innermost hearts, as though we know what only God can know.

How can the struggle with a temptation have any benefit? In order to see this we must first learn to recognize judging thoughts just as we would any other distracting thought and work it into our contemplative practice. The first step, then, is not magically to decide somehow to avoid judgmental thoughts, but to catch ourselves in the act. So bring them on.

If we have some skill with the riddles of distraction discussed in a previous chapter—meeting thoughts with stillness and not commentary—we will quickly gain a sense of this.

Let the presence of a judgmental thought become a reminder to return to our practice. If we are practicing with the riddles of the First Doorway, then the momentum of these judgmental thoughts will be considerable; so we brace ourselves for an ordeal and a fair amount of defeat. But gradually and with much patience a threshold will be crossed, and we will be able to embrace with silent awareness our judgmental thought. We let the judgmental thought be and release ourselves into our prayer word instead of getting caught up in the narrative of the judgmental thought. This is easier said than done, but with practice the tables begin to turn. The temptation to sin is itself disclosing an invitation to prayer, and we are being deepened more than derailed by this very trial.

At no time are we trying to push away our judging thoughts. Nor do we indulge them by getting caught up in their narrative. Instead we "look over their shoulder," as the author of *The Cloud of Unknowing* tells us, "Try to look over their shoulders, as it were, searching for something else—and that something is God, enclosed in a cloud of unknowing."[9] There is a certain genius in his advice: in order to look over their shoulders we have to let the judgmental thoughts be, but we won't be able to look over their shoulders if we get wrapped up in the narrative of the judgmental thoughts.

When this judgmental thought is thoroughly worked into our practice and brought "into captivity to Christ" (2 Cor 10:5), it is playing an entirely new role. Previously it was an obstacle that led us astray. Now it is offering us its shoulder to steady our gaze into the luminous vastness that is the ground of all. We cite Eckhart's observation again. "What was previously an obstacle to you is now a great help."[10] When worked into our practice temptation becomes something like resistance training; it works against the direction we would like to go in, but if engaged in the right way, it strengthens us.

Meeting the temptation to judge others in this way can lead us to a liberating breakthrough. The vision of our inner eye broadens and deepens. We will see more clearly what place temptation plays in the circuitry of our struggles; how judgmental thoughts are a mass of anger, fear, envy, pride, and shame; in what measure our specific struggles involve an inclination to sin, or are simply wounds of personal history, or the fingerprint of character. Often there is less sin and transgression than we thought previously. The eye that sees all this is the eye of compassion that is born of silence.

One of the most precious things we learn is noncondemnation. When we see the judgmental thoughts finally disappear in the ground of awareness, much of what had seemed worthy of condemnation now seems just right the way it is. Whether our own or those of others, imperfections are seen to manifest the same ineffable vastness as virtues do. These same imperfections may be considerable indeed and pose a real obstacle; yet there is no need to condemn. Thorns are as much a part of a rose as the flower. What gardener condemns the compost for being full of rubbish?

MUSIC BEHIND THE DOOR OF DESPAIR: HUMILITY AND FAILURE

Humility is necessary if we are to see into our wounds. However, one of obstacles to the discovery of the Divine Presence, that is the ground of even our wounds, is that we easily get caught in judging our own faults and failings. By this I do not mean we should not be able to admit fault, confess failings, make amends. Indeed we should. I'm saying that we get *caught* in this. Even when there is no question of sin or transgression, many people are entangled in a snare of self-loathing and are constantly running themselves down. Somehow we come to believe that we are simply not adequate; that we can never be good enough. Sometimes this self-loathing masquerades as a compulsive need to blame others for things that go wrong; for any suggestion that we might have made a mistake is simply too threatening an indictment. The problem is that this is just another mind game. Self-loathing is just another video we've learned to watch. This actually is an obstacle to the humility required to see straight through our wounds into God. For true humility is the wide open space of self-knowledge that opens onto God.

The author of *The Cloud of Unknowing* defines humility as "a true knowledge and feeling of oneself as one is."[11] This involves all our faults and failings, "humanity's impurity, wretchedness and weakness, into which we have fallen by sin, and which we must always feel to some degree while we live on earth, however holy we may be."[12] Interestingly, however, the author of *The Cloud* calls this "imperfect humility." He says there are two types of humility, perfect and imperfect, and the awareness of all our faults and failings is what he calls "imperfect humility." What, then, is perfect humility?

The author has said humility is true self-knowledge. He gives a key insight into what this self-knowledge entails at the beginning of *The Book of Privy Counselling*. He says God "is your being, and you are what you are in him."[13] Self-knowledge cannot end in the awareness of our faults and failings. It opens onto God. The author of the *The Cloud* says this perfect humility is caused by "the superabundant love and excellence of God in himself, at the sight of which all nature trembles, all scholars are fools, and all saints and angels are blind."[14] Perfect humility is meeting the unfathomable love of God, who is the ground of our being.

How does imperfect humility become perfect humility? The author of *The Cloud* says, "The soul will suddenly and completely lose and forget all knowledge and feeling of its existence, paying no attention to whether it has been holy or wretched. During this time it is made perfectly humble, for it knows and feels no reason but the chief one."[15] In order for humility to mature it must blossom into self-forgetfulness.

This advice is especially valuable for people with a high sense of sin or who struggle with self-loathing or the inability to forgive themselves. Very often we think we've got to keep all this ever in mind. While awareness of sin and transgression has its place, it must nevertheless be set aside if growth in humility is to continue. The author is aware that incessant rehearsing of our faults and failings, is just another mind game, more inner chatter that keeps the ego center stage. Humility is perfect, he says, "when its goal is God alone." Humility is imperfect "when its goal is anything else mixed with God (even if God is the chief goal)." So if we are caught up in the stories we tell ourselves about our transgressions, this is clearly imperfect humility; for there is something else going on other than silent communion with God. While the author of *The Cloud* sees the importance of imperfect humility as a necessary element, by itself it is insufficient.

What is more humble than awareness of sin? For the author of *The Cloud*, our contemplative practice is an act of perfect humility. For "this spiritual exercise excels all other exercises, spiritual or bodily, that one can or may engage in by grace—how a secret thrust of love, directed in purity of spirit at this dark cloud of unknowing between you and your God, subtly and completely contains within it the perfect virtue of humility."[16] We have to let go of everything, even our sense of being a miserable failure.

Clearly the author has no problem with humility involving sorrow for sin. "Do not think," he says, "because I mention two reasons for humility, one perfect and another imperfect, that I therefore want you to give up working towards imperfect humility and apply yourself wholly to achieving perfect humility. No, indeed, I believe you would never succeed in that way."[17] He is, however, concerned that sorrow for sins be not co-opted by our mind games, which can take the form of inability to trust in our fundamental goodness, inability to believe that divine love doesn't have to decide whether or not to forgive. Divine love *is* forgiving love. Sorrow must be allowed to blossom into self-forgetful love of God. The author is no doubt aware that our mind games are very subtle and have great momentum; they are the problem, not the sorrow. According to the author of *The Cloud* the gospel figure, Mary Magdalene, got this exactly right.

For centuries the figure of Mary Magdalene had been identified with the un-named repentant sinner (Lk 7:37). Though today we know this is not the case, the author of *The Cloud* was very much a part of this way of interpreting her. Nevertheless there remains much of great value in his reflection on her. What impresses him about Mary Magdalene is not how she changed her ways and experienced true sorrow and forgiveness. This he presumes. What intrigues him is how she was transfigured from dedicated sinner to a woman of deep prayer.

He claims she did not allow memories of past misdeeds to get in the way of silent communion with God. He tells his reader that she did not get caught up in "sorting through her sins one by one in every detail, and sorrowing and weeping for each of them separately."[18] Not because she had not truly repented but because "she was more likely to have aroused in herself the possibility of sinning again than to have obtained complete forgiveness of all her sins."[19] Here the author shows his psychological astuteness as he puts his finger on the pulse of a problem many people have.

It is not uncommon to find people with very sensitive consciences and who seem to have a certain attraction, even aptitude, for the contemplative path, but who cannot come to terms with things that have happened in their past. Not only can they not accept divine forgiveness, they cannot forgive themselves. Consequently their self-esteem is too low to accept the fact that failure is part of the search for God. As Eckhart says of all the saints and sages down through history, "We rarely find people who achieve great things without first going astray."[20] But such wisdom is little comfort to these individuals. This preoccupation with sin can become a type of obsessive-compulsive disorder (in former times this was called scrupulosity), which increases the likelihood of sliding back into the same old problems. According to the author of *The Cloud*, if you are constantly obsessing on what you've done and frightened that it might happen again, it is more likely to happen again, than if you could simply come to terms with it and move on.

In a similar context Meister Eckhart distinguishes two kinds of repentance. He says that there is a kind of repentance that "draws us downwards into yet greater suffering, plunging us into such distress that it is as if we were already in a state of despair. And so repentance can find no way out of suffering. Nothing comes of this."[21] Eckhart contrasts this kind of repentance with the repentance "which is of God" and says that it "brings spiritual joy that lifts the soul out of her suffering and distress and binds her to God."[22] It becomes a question of dealing with afflictive thoughts in the right way. This was the key to Mary Magdalene's success; she was able to break the cycle of obsessive thinking. How did she do this? He says "she hung her love and her longing desire on this cloud of unknowing."[23] By this he means she simply returned to her prayer word rather than to the obsessive thinking. In doing this she discovers perfect humility.

In his poem, "From Failure Up," Patrick Kavanagh asks:

> O God: can a man find you when he lies with his face
> downwards
> And his nose in the rubble that was his achievement?
> Is the music playing behind the door of despair?[24]

Those who speak from experience of the contemplative path know, as the poet himself may have known, what lies behind this door. Upholding all struggle, failure, brokenness is the Living God who embraces humanity where it stands most in need. The practice of contemplation will lead us to this door. The contemplative learns that this is precisely where practice leads us and where we learn to listen, not to confusing shrills of despair, but to "the music behind the door of despair."

A mature contemplative practice places us squarely before the wound of the human condition, and we learn to meet our wounds in a new way. At first this is difficult, and there is great resistance. But gradually we learn something very precious under the tutelage of these wounds. We learn a compassion for others that replaces judging, self-loathing, and the compulsion to find someone to blame. We learn a reverent joy before our wounds that replaces the condemnation of and comparison of ourselves with others that used to fuel our anxiety. We learn that the consummation of self-esteem is self-forgetful abandonment to the Silence of God that gives birth to loving service of all who struggle.

What could we have learned without the help of our wounds, our brokenness, our failure? They have been the source of so much wisdom. Julian of Norwich says, "Although a man has the scars of healed wounds, when he appears before God they do not deface but ennoble him."[25] Our wounds are our trophies.

Our own interior silence will have solved many riddles and opened many doorways before we can stare failure in the face and see not our own face but God's. In the Crucified and Risen One, grace and disgrace have been joined. Because of this, our failure opens onto the luminous vastness of our depths, where Christ silently presides in the unfolding liturgy of our wounds.

Epilogue

"Who am I?" A Tale of Monastic Failure

Abba Poemen said to Abba Joseph, "Tell me how to become a monk." He said, "If you want to find rest here below, and here-after, in all circumstances say, Who am I? and do not judge anyone."

—Sayings of the Desert Fathers

PART ONE

There was once a young man who didn't have the foggiest notion of what he wanted to do with his life. One day he said to himself, "I know what. I'll enter a monastery, but not just any monastery. I want to enter a *real* monastery. So off he went determined to find a real monastery. He came to the first monastery he could find and knocked on the door. The porter answered the door and said to the young man, "Good afternoon. How may I help you?"

The young man said, "I'd like to enter a monastery, but it's got to be a *real* monastery. Is this a *real* monastery?"

The porter towered over him and pierced him with his dark eyes. He said to the young man, "I'm sure you'd be more than welcome here, but I'm afraid I shall have to tell you we're not a real monastery at all. We're a fake monastery, you see. We're only pretending. So if you've got your heart set on a real monastery, I'm afraid you'll have to carry on down the road a bit until you come to the real monastery. You'll come to it before long. Now off with you. There's a good fella."

The young man was delighted. He bade the porter farewell and set off down the road to find the real monastery. Soon he came to a large sign pointing down a small road that led into the woods. The sign read, "Real Monastery 100 Yards." Rubbing his hands in excitement, he followed the little road into the woods.

He knocked on the door, and the porter of the monastery soon answered. "Good afternoon. How may I help you?" The young man's jaw dropped in amazement. He was certain it was the very same monk who was the porter at the fake monastery just up the road. The young man said, "I'd like to enter a *real* monastery."

The porter clasped his hands together and said, "Well, you've come to the right place. Just come right in, and I'll take you down to the novitiate. I'm sure something can be arranged." On the way the porter explained to the young man how fortunate he was not to have fallen for that fake monastery up the road.

The young man settled into the novitiate with relative ease. He found he liked all his fellow novices and pretty much all the monks he came across. It wasn't long before he felt certain he wanted to stay here for the rest of his days. So he went to the novice master and said, "I believe I'm ready to make my profession." The novice master said, "Well, the abbot will have to see you about this."

In due course an appointment with the abbot was arranged, and the young man sat down to speak with the abbot about his vocation. The abbot asked him why he felt he was ready to make his profession. The young man said, "Well, I've come to like it here very much. Everyone is nice to me, and I like all the monks."

The abbot said, "Well, that is very encouraging to hear, and I'd have to say that we are very happy to have you and we hope that you stay. But just the same, I think you should go back to the novitiate for a while longer. It'll do you no harm."

The young man left in great distress. Why didn't the abbot want him to make his profession? Did he say something wrong? Was he deluded about his vocation? Not a little disappointed, the young man returned to his life as a novice. The abbot's gentle rebuff ended up teaching the young man a great deal about his own faults and failings and presumption. He began to grow in self-knowledge and applied himself with great dedication to the study of the monastery's long history, its traditions, and various customs. He soon mastered all of this.

After more than a year the young man was convinced that now he would be able to answer correctly any question the abbot might put to him and he could see, moreover, the abbot's wisdom in putting him off for a time. And so the young man told the novice master that he felt he was now ready to make his profession and could he please see the abbot. The novice master arranged this, and soon enough the young man was brought to the abbot.

The abbot said, "I'm very happy to hear that you still want to make your profession and to live out your monastic life among us. But tell me, why do you feel you are ready to make your profession?"

The young man responded, "I'm convinced that this is what God is asking of me. I don't claim to understand it. I only know it is something I must do. Moreover, I have been studying our tradition and our charism. I identify with it very deeply and think it confirms the sense of interior call that I feel."

The abbot was obviously listening to him very intently and sincerely. He said to the young man, "What you say is very edifying indeed, and I feel even myself encouraged in the life just listening to you speak the way you do about your conviction of God's love for you and of his call. But I think you should go back to the novitiate, back to the novitiate until you are really ready."

The man was in quite a state as he left the abbot's office. He was in fact completely shattered. He couldn't imagine what on earth the abbot could possibly have wanted to hear. He knew he belonged more in the monastery than half of those other wretched monks. But he returned to the novitiate. He had already completed his formal studies, so he took to helping in the garden, pruning vines and thinning carrots and also served in the infirmary.

He carried on with these jobs for what seemed like years. One day the abbot asked the novice master, "What about that man who was so intent on making his profession in our monastery. Is he no longer interested?"

"He doesn't mention it much any more," said the novice master.

"Is he unhappy?" asked the abbot.

"No, he seems content enough," responded the novice master. "He doesn't say much to anyone. He goes about his tasks in the garden; he consoles the old monks in the infirmary, and encourages the new ones in the novitiate."

"Bring him to me," said the abbot.

The man was brought to he abbot who began to question him: "I was wondering if you were still interested in making your profession. You don't seem as keen to do it as you once were when you were making such a thorough study of our tradition. Have you gone off the idea altogether?"

The man looked at the abbot. The lines beginning to show round the man's eyes reflected the fact that he'd been in the monastery a number of years now. But his face had the freshness and peace of those whose poverty had taught them they had nothing to defend. The man said to the abbot, "Jesus Christ is my monastery."

The abbot sat up in his chair and leaned forward. He gazed into the man as though looking for something, looked into him as though gazing into the heart of mystery. His gaze fixed on the man, sifting him, assessing every turn taken, every decision made in order to know if this man really knew what he had said. The abbot stood up slowly, towered over him and said, "You have learned our tradition well. May I have your blessing?"

PART TWO

After this man's second request for profession had been turned down and the abbot had sent him back to the novitiate until he was truly ready, he was in complete despair. This last rejection had unleashed within him a flood of swirling anxiety. He was seen working quietly around the place, but in fact he was only keeping up appearances; underneath his novice robes were spasms of chaos that would assault him like pounding waves. Once the chaos within was churning, it was all he could do to keep putting one foot in front of the other and somehow just manage to hold on. When the spasms of chaos let up, he would merely try to catch his breath and hope against hope that this was the last of these tidal waves of fear and panic. But it never was. Weeks became months. He realized he needed help, but to whom could he go? The novice master was allergic to life, and his regular confessor was completely switched off. There were 150 monks in the monastery. Who could help him? A certain Fr. Alypius eventually came to mind.

Fr. Alypius was something of a maverick, but he was thought to be wise. He was the cobbler and more or less lived in his little shop down at the bottom of the garden. He rarely spoke to anyone. It was said that he could read people's hearts, so everyone stayed away. The young man said to himself, "I've got to go to him." The next day at prayers, he left a note in Fr. Alypius's place in chapel. "Can I talk to you about something?" By early afternoon he got his reply. "Come to me this evening after supper." So after supper he crept down to the bottom of the garden to speak with Fr. Alypius.

Crouched over a table, Fr. Alypius was sitting on a stool repairing someone's shoes. He peered over the top of his spectacles and said, "Sit down and tell me what's wrong."

The young man went on for an eternity. He told him everything about his life, about his search for a real monastery, about his refusal for profession. All the while Fr. Alypius was working away on this one shoe. When the young man had finished, Fr. Alypius said, "I have just one question for you: 'who are you?'"

"I just told you," said the young man.

"No, you told me about the clothes you wear. You told me your name, where you're from, what you've done, the things you've studied. Your problem is, you don't know who you are. Let me tell you who you are. You are a ray of God's own light."

"Sounds a bit silly," the young man thought to himself. But he was intrigued, so he said, "What do you mean?"

"You say you seek God, but a ray of light doesn't seek the sun; it's coming from the sun. You are a branch on the vine of God. A branch doesn't seek the vine; it's already part of the vine. A wave doesn't look for the ocean; it's already full of ocean. Because you don't know that who you are is one with God, you believe all these labels about yourself: I'm a sinner, I'm a saint, I'm a wretch, I'm a worm and no man, I'm a monk, I'm a nurse. These are all labels, clothing. They serve a purpose, but they are not who you are. To the extent that you believe these labels, you believe a lie, and you add anguish upon anguish. It's what most of us do for most of our lives. In the secular world we call it our career. In monastic terms, we call it our vocation."

"Before you can know in your own experience what the Psalmist meant when he said, 'Be still and know that I am God,' you must first learn to be still and know who you are. The rest will follow."

Then Fr. Alypius said, "Tell me about your prayer."

"Well I never miss the community prayers," the young man replied.

"I didn't ask you about saying your prayers. I asked about *prayer.*"

"Do you mean silent prayer?"

"Tell me about that."

"I have trouble being silent," said the young man.

"But you already are silent. I understand how there is a lot of noise and chaos swirling around. That's true of us all. But you, *you* are silence. You are the silence that is aware of the chaos. You are the silence that sees the chaos. Again, I tell you, you don't know who you are."

"What's all this chaos then?" asked the young man.

"It's just weather. Tell me, what happens when you sit in silence?"

"I try to give myself over to contemplation and then get lost in thoughts."

"But silence," Fr. Alypius said, "silence and contemplation are concerned with what is deeper than thinking, with that vastness in which the things going on in your head appear. When this vastness full of vibrant emptiness is recognized to be the center of all appearances, even the inner chaos, then it becomes obvious that contemplation, silence, is always present."

"I think I've glimpsed something of this, but normally I'm just lost in my thoughts," confessed the young man.

"Are you? I thought you were a ray of God's own light, a branch on the vine. Now you say you are something different. You say you are someone lost in thoughts. But isn't this thought, 'I am lost in my thoughts,' just another thought, just another label that is being believed? We assume we are our thoughts, but look and see. Are *you* lost in your thoughts?"

"Not right now. But if I went back and tried to sit in silence, there would just be this inner chatter. I know my mind should be quiet. I should be having no thoughts."

Fr. Alypius continued his instruction, "These new thoughts: 'my mind should be quiet'; 'I shouldn't be having thoughts,' are noisier than the previous thoughts. But these particular thoughts are believed to be the truth. Believing them to be the truth distracts you from the deeper reality. Silence is naturally present. Silence cannot *not* be there. When you think, 'I'm lost in my thoughts; my mind should be silent,' just stop for a second and ask: '*Who* is lost? *Who* is not quiet?' Do it right now."

There was a pause. The young man looked hard.

Fr. Alypius asked him, "When you look directly into the thought do you see someone who is lost?"

"No, there is no one there. There is no one who is lost. In that moment there is not a chatterer, but then that moment is gone and all the chatter comes back."

"That's right," cheered Fr. Alypius. "Thoughts keep coming back because that's just what thoughts do. But if you look directly at the thought or feeling and ask who is the chatterer, who is suffering, you won't find anybody, you won't find a sufferer. There will be chattering, sure. Suffering, sure. The thoughts coming and going. Don't look at the suffering, the anguish, the fear. These are objects of awareness. I'm asking you to look into the awareness itself. Not the objects of awareness. These have dominated your attention for decades. Let your attention rest in the awareness, not the objects of awareness. Yes, I can see on your face. The mind grows still. Tell me what do you see?"

"Nothing," said the young man. "Just this vast nothing."

"Tell me, what is the substance of all this chatter and chaos in your head?"

The young man responded, "It's just fluff."

"That's right," said Fr. Alypius. "Do you see how simple it is? It is not special or rarefied. It's not because you've been chanting for nine hours straight or fasting for the last three weeks. These monastic strategies are of no use because it has already been accomplished. When you see that you are caught up in the storms of chaos, inner chatter, and mental commentary, ask yourself, 'Who am I?' Ask '*Who* is experiencing the chaos? *Who* is chattering? *Who* is the commentator?' You won't find anyone there checking to see if you are caught in thoughts. When you turn your attention from the object of your awareness to the awareness itself, there is just silent, vast, openness that has never been wounded, harmed, angry, frightened, incomplete. This is who you are."

On many evenings the young man would make his way down to the bottom of the garden for conversations with Fr. Alypius. They were all about the question, "Who am I?" The young man grew in wisdom and in this paradox of identity, and there was a great calm about him. On their final meeting Fr. Alypius said, "You have mastered the question 'Who am I?' I would like to put to you another question: 'Who is Jesus Christ?'" The young man was fixed in a silent, inner gaze. As he looked at the young man, Fr. Alypius's face brightened; he could see that the young man knew. He sat back and returned to repairing a shoe and said to the young man. "Well done. Now off with you. I believe the abbot wants to have a word with you."

Notes

INTRODUCTION

1. Leo Tolstoy, *The Death of Ivan Ilyich*, trans. L. Solotaroff (New York: Bantam Books, 1981), 133–134.
2. St. Augustine, *The City of God*, IX, 17, trans. H. Bettenson (Harmondsworth, UK: Penguin Books, 1972), 364. Augustine is probably quoting Plotinus, *Ennead* I.6.8.
3. St. John of the Cross, *Maxims on Love*, 21, in *The Collected Works of St. John of the Cross*, trans. K. Kavanaugh and O. Rodriguez (Washington, DC: Institute of Carmelite Studies Publications, 1979), 675.
4. St. John of the Cross, Letter Seven, in *The Collected Works of St. John of the Cross*, 689.
5. Maggie Ross, *The Fountain and the Furnace: The Way of Tears and Fire* (Mahwah, NJ: Paulist Press, 1987), 17.
6. St. John of the Cross, *The Ascent of Mount Carmel*, in *The Collected Works of St. John of the Cross*, 67.
7. Pauline Matarasso, *The Price of Admission* (Cambridge: Broughton House Books, 2005), 72.
8. St. Augustine, *On the Trinity*, VIII, 7, 11, (translation my own).

9. R. S. Thomas, "AD," in *Collected Later Poems 1988–2000* (Tarset, Northumberland, UK: Bloodaxe Books, 2004), 118.

O N E

1. See Elaine MacInnes, "Light Behind Bars," *The Tablet*, 17 August 1996, 1071–72.

2. St. Augustine, *Confessions*, III, 6, (translation my own).

3. Ibid., X, 27, (translation my own).

4. *The Book of Privy Counselling*, chap. 1 in *The Cloud of Unknowing and Other Works*, trans. A. C. Spearing (Harmondsworth, UK: Penguin, 2001), 104, (translation altered slightly).

5. Ibid., (translation altered slightly).

6. St. John of the Cross, *The Living Flame of Love*, I, 12, in K. Kavanaugh and O. Rodriguez, trans., *The Collected Works of St. John of the Cross* (Washington, DC: Institute of Carmelite Studies Publications, 1979), 583.

7. St. Diadochos of Photiki, *On Spiritual Knowledge*, 9, quoted in *The Philokalia*, vol. I, trans. G. Palmer, P. Sherrard, and K. Ware (London: Faber and Faber, 1979), 255.

8. St. John of the Cross, *The Ascent Mount Carmel*, II, chap. 5, 3, in *The Collected Works of St. John of the Cross*, 116.

9. See *The Book of Privy Counselling*, chap. 1, 104, (translation altered slightly).

10. St. Augustine, *Confessions*, I, 1, (translation my own).

11. An ancient description of God that goes as far back as Hermes Trismegistis and is famously cited by Blaise Pascal, *Pensées*, 119, trans. A. J. Krailsheimer (Harmondsworth, UK: Penguin, 1995), 60.

12. This verse is subsequently incorporated into the Roman Catholic Church's Eucharistic Preface VI for Sundays in Ordinary Time.

13. St. Augustine, Sermon 272 (CCLXXII), On the Feast of Pentecost, in J. P. Migne, ed., *Patrologia Latina*, 38, 1247, (translation my own).

14. John Ruysbroeck, *Flowers of a Mystic Garden* (London: Watkins, 1912; reprinted Llanerch Publishers, 1994), 69–70.

15. Elaine MacInnes, "Light Behind Bars," 1072.

16. Meister Eckhart, Sermon 25, in *Meister Eckhart: Selected Writings*, trans. and ed. O. Davies (Harmondsworth, UK: Penguin, 1994), 228.

17. St. John of the Cross, *The Living Flame of Love*, II, 10, in *The Collected Works of St. John of the Cross*, 599.

18. Meister Eckhart, Sermon 16, in *Meister Eckhart: Selected Writings*, 179.

19. St. John of the Cross, *The Spiritual Canticle*, Red A., str. 38. I have taken this translation from an older version of The Liturgy of the Hours, Office of Readings for the memorial of St. John of the Cross, 14 December.

TWO

1. "You have no need of our praise, but the desire to thank you is itself your gift" (Roman Catholic Eucharistic Preface IV for Weekdays in Ordinary Time).

2. R. S. Thomas, "The Moor," in *Collected Poems 1945–1990* (London: Dent, 1993), 166.

3. R. S. Thomas, "The Untamed," in *Collected Poems 1945–1990*, 140.

4. See St. Augustine, *Confessions*, IX, 10.

5. St. John Climacus, *The Ladder of Divine Ascent*, Step 11, 4 (5), trans. C. Luibheid and N. Russell (Mahwah, NJ: Paulist Press, 1982), 159.

6. Meister Eckhart, Sermon I, in *Sermons and Treatises*, vol. I, trans. M. Walshe (Longmead, Shaftsbury, UK: Element Books, 1979), 6–7.

7. St. John of the Cross, *Maxims on Love*, 21, in *The Collected Works of St. John of the Cross*, trans. K. Kavanaugh and R. Rodriguez (Washington, DC: Institute of Carmelite Studies, 1979), 675.

8. Angelus Silesius, *The Cherubinic Wanderer*, I, 240, trans. M. Shrady, Classics of Western Spirituality (Mahwah, NJ: Paulist Press, 1986), 49.

9. St. Augustine, Letter 130, 15, 28 in *The Works of Saint Augustine* II/2, trans. R. Teske (Hyde Park, NY: New City Press, 2003), 197.

10. Charles Dickens, *Hard Times* (Harmondsworth, UK: Penguin Books, 1985), 47.

11. St. Augustine, *On the Trinity*, XII, 1.

12. Evagrius, *Chapters on Prayer*, chap. 3, in *The Praktikos and Chapters on Prayer*, trans. J. Bamberger (Kalamazoo, MI: Cistercian Publications, 1981), 56, (translation altered slightly).

13. St. Thomas Aquinas, *Summa Theologiae*, 1a q. 79, a. 9.

14. Dante, *The Divine Comedy, Paradise*, 2, 56–57, trans. A. Mandelbaum (New York: A. Knopf, 1984).

15. Quoted in Chariton's *The Art of Prayer*, trans. E. Kadloubovsky and E. Palmer (London: Faber and Faber, 1966), 183.

16. Theophan cited in *The Art of Prayer*, 183.

17. R. S. Thomas, "The Untamed," in *Collected Poems 1945–1990*, 140.

18. St. Augustine, *Exposition of the Psalms*, 76, 9 in *The Works of Saint Augustine* III/18, trans. M. Boulding (Hyde Park, NY: New City Press, 2002), 81.

19. St. Augustine, *Confessions* X, 27, (translation my own).

THREE

1. George Eliot, *Adam Bede* (Harmondsworth, UK: Penguin, 1980), 202.

2. C. S. Lewis, *The Screwtape Letters*, IV (New York: MacMillan, 1961), 25.

3. James Joyce, "A Painful Case" in *The Dubliners* (New York: Bantam Books, 1990), 84.

4. St. John Climacus, *Ladder of Divine Ascent*, 27; see *The Philokalia* vol. IV, trans. G. Palmer, P. Sherrard, and K. Ware (London: Faber and Faber, 1995), 336.

5. Evagrius, "On Discrimination," chap. 14, *The Philokalia*, vol. I, trans. G. Palmer, P. Sherrard, and K. Ware (London: Faber and Faber, 1979) 47.

6. R. S. Thomas, "Adam Tempted," in *Collected Later Poems 1988–2000* (Tarset, Northumberland, UK: Bloodaxe Books), 141.

7. St. Maximus the Confessor, *Scholia on The Divine Names*, PG 4, 208 C. See Jn 4:24. "God is spirit." Cited in Olivier Clément, *The Roots of Christian Mysticism*, trans. T. Berkeley (London: New City Press, 1993), 33. The Greek word translated into English as "spirit" is *pneuma*, which can also mean "breath."

8. Theophilus of Antioch, *Three Books to Autolycus*, I, 7, cited in Olivier Clément, *The Roots of Christian Mysticism*, trans. T. Berkeley (London: New City Press, 1993), 73.

9. St. John of the Cross, *The Spiritual Canticle*, Red A., str. 38. I have taken this translation from an older version of *The Liturgy of the Hours*, Office of Readings for the memorial of St. John of the Cross, 14 December.

10. Cited in Antoine Guillamont, "The Jesus Prayer among the Monks of Egypt," *The Eastern Churches Review*, 6 (1974), 66–71 at 67.

11. While Marcarius and Evagrius are fourth century, this story only survives in a Coptic version dating from the ninth century.

12. St. John Climacus, *The Ladder of Divine Ascent*, chap. 27, trans. C. Luibheid and N. Russell (Mahwah, NJ: Paulist Press, 1982), 270.

13. St. Hesychios, *On Watchfulness and Holiness*, chap. 182, in *The Philokalia*, vol. I, 195.

14. *On Watchfulness*, chap. 189, in *The Philokalia*, vol. I, 196.

15. Ibid., chap. 187, 195.

16. St. Gregory Palamas, *Those who Practice a Life of Stillness*, chap. 7, in *The Philokalia*, vol. IV, 337.

17. Nicephorus the Solitary, *A Most Profitable Discourse on Sobriety and the Guarding of the Heart*, in *Writings from the Philokalia on Prayer of the Heart*, trans. E. Kadloubovsky and G. Palmer (London: Faber and Faber, 1951), 33.

18. Ibid.

19. Callistus and Ignatius, *Directions to Hesychasts*, chap. 45, in *Writings from the Philokalia on Prayer of the Heart*, 220; see also chaps. 19 and 20, 192–193.

20. *Directions to Hesychasts*, chap. 24, in *Writings from the Philokalia on Prayer of the Heart*, 195.

21. Ibid.

22. *The Art of Prayer: An Orthodox Anthology*, compiled by Igumen Chariton, trans. E. Kadloubovsky and E. Palmer (London: Faber and Faber, 1966), 96–97, see also 103.

23. Ibid., 104.

24. Ibid., 98.

25. Lorenzo Scudi, *Unseen Warfare*, trans. E. Kadloubovsky and G. Palmer (London: Faber and Faber, 1952), 205.

26. Gregory of Sinai, *On Stillness*, 2–3, in *The Philokalia*, vol. IV, 264–265.

27. R. S. Thomas, "The Moor," in *Collected Poems 1945–1990* (London: J. M. Dent, 1993), 166.

28. R. S. Thomas, "AD," in *Collected Later Poems: 1988–2000* (Tarset, Northumberland, UK: Bloodaxe Books, 2004), 118.

FOUR

1. J. D. Salinger, *Franny and Zooey* (Boston: Little, Brown and Company, 1961), 29–30.

2. *Maxims on Love*, 9, in *The Collected Works of St. John of the Cross*, trans. K. Kavanaugh and O. Rodriguez (Washington, DC: Institute of Carmelite Studies Publications, 1979), 674.

3. Evagrius, *Antirrhetikos*, Prologue, in *Evagrius Ponticus*, ed. and trans. W. Frankenberg (Berlin, 1912), 472–473, trans. M. O'Laughlin in V. Wimbush, ed., *Ascetic Behavior in Greco-Roman Antiquity: A Sourcebook*, Studies in Antiquity and Christianity (Minneapolis: Fortress Press, 1990), 243–262.

4. St. Diadochos of Photiki, "On Spiritual Knowledge," chap. 59 in *The Philokalia*, trans. G. Palmer, P. Sherrard, and K. Ware (London: Faber and Faber, 1979), vol. I, 270.

5. Sermon 8, On the Third Commandment, in *The Works of St. Augustine* III/1, trans. E. Hill (Brooklyn, NY: New City Press), 244.

6. Quoted in Douglas Burton-Christie, "Hunger," *Spiritus* 5, 2 (2005), vii.

7. St. Augustine, Sermon 169, 13, trans. Edmond Hill, *Sermons*, *The Works of Saint Augustine*, III/1 (New Rochelle, NY: New City Press, 1992), 231.

8. St. Teresa of Avila, *The Interior Castle*, V, 2, trans. M. Star, (New York: Riverhead Books, 2003), 126.

9. Ibid., 127–130.

10. Ibid., 129.

11. St. Augustine, Letter 130 in *The Works of Saint Augustine* II/ 2, trans. R. Teske (Hyde Park, NY: New City Press, 2003), 193.

12. Evagrius, *Antirrheticus*, V, trans. M. O'Laughlin in V. Wimbush, ed., *Ascetic Behavior in Greco-Roman Antiquity: A Sourcebook*, 257.

13. Evagrius, *Antirrheticus*, IV, in ibid., 256.

14. See John Cassian, Conference 9 and 10, in *John Cassian: Conferences*, trans. C. Luibheid and N. Russell (Mahwah, NJ: Paulist Press, 1985).

15. *The Cloud of Unknowing*, trans. A. C. Spearing, (Harmondsworth, UK: Penguin Classics, 2001), chap. 7, 29.

16. Thomas Keating, *Open Mind, Open Heart: The Contemplative Dimension of the Gospel* (New York: Crossroad, 2001); John Main, *Word into Silence* (London: Darton, Longman and Todd, 1980).

17. *The Art of Prayer: An Orthodox Anthology*, compiled by Igumen Chariton (London: Faber and Faber, 1966), 99–100.

18. Ibid., 99.

19. *Franny and Zooey*, 37.

20. *The Art of Prayer*, 90–91.

21. Ibid.

22. *Open Mind, Open Heart*, 93–107.

23. *The Art of Prayer*, 100.

24. Ibid., 101.

25. Thanks to Mary Jane Rubenstein for the term "unselfed self."

26. "On Spiritual Knowledge," chap. 4, in *The Philokalia*, vol. I, 253.

27. Ibid., chap. 59, 270.

28. St. John of the Cross, *The Living Flame of Love*, I, 26, in *The Collected Works of St. John of the Cross*, 589.

29. Geoffrey Hill, "The Pentecost Castle, 13," in *Collected Poems* (London: André Deutsch, 1986), 143.

30. Dante, *Paradiso*, XXXIII, 145, trans. A. Mandelbaum (New York: A. Knopf, 1984).

31. "On Spiritual Knowledge," chap. 97, in *The Philokalia*, vol. I, 294.

32. John Chapman, *Spiritual Letters* (London: Sheed and Ward, 1935), 108.

FIVE

1. St. Teresa of Avila, *The Interior Castle*, IV, 3, trans. M. Starr (New York: Riverhead Books, 2004), 107.

2. Evagrius, *The Praktikos*, chap. 50, in *The Praktikos and Chapters on Prayer*, trans. J. Bamberger (Kalamazoo, MI: Cistercian Publications, 1981), 29–30

3. Ibid., chap. 43, 28.

4. Ibid., chap. 54, 31.

5. John Chapman, *Spiritual Letters* (London: Sheed and Ward, 1935), 52–53.

6. See Gerald May, *Will and Spirit: Toward a Contemplative Psychology* (New York: Harper and Row, 1982), 112–113.

7. St. Gregory of Nyssa, Homily Five in *Commentary on the Song of Songs*, trans. C. McCambley (Brookline, MA: Hellenic College Press, 1987), 119, (translation altered).

8. *The Cloud of Unknowing*, chap. 32, in *The Cloud of Unknowing and Other Works*, trans. A. C. Spearing (Harmondsworth, UK: Penguin, 2001), 55.

9. Evagrius, *Praktikos*, chap. 54, 34.

SIX

1. Barry Lopez, *Arctic Dreams: Imagination and Desire in a Northern Landscape* (New York: Bantam Books, 1987), 97–98. My thanks to Martha Reeves for pointing me to this book.

2. Evagrius, *Praktikos*, chap. 50 in *The Praktikos and Chapters on Prayer*, trans. J. Bamberger (Kalamazoo, MI: Cistercian Publications, 1981), 29–30.

3. See *Praktikos*, chap. 43, 28.

4. Hesychios, *On Watchfulness and Holiness*, chap. 5, in *The Philokalia*, vol. I, trans. G. Palmer, P. Sherrard, and K. Ware (London: Faber and Faber, 1979), 163.

5. *On Watchfulness*, chap. 14, in *The Philokalia*, vol. I, 164.

6. Ibid., chaps. 15 and 16, 164–165.

7. Meister Eckhart, Sermon 25 in *Meister Eckhart: Selected Writings*, trans. and ed. O. Davies (Harmondsworth, UK: Penguin Books, 1994), 228.

8. St. Teresa of Avila, *The Interior Castle*, I, 2, trans. M. Starr (New York: Riverhead Books, 2003), 47–48.

9. Ibid., 41.

10. *On Watchfulness*, chap. 7, in *The Philokalia*, vol. I, 163, (translation altered slightly).

11. Simone Weil, *Gravity and Grace* (London: Routledge and Kegan Paul, 1963), 132.

12. *Chapters on Prayer*, chap. 44, 62.

13. *Chapters on Prayer*, chap. 46, 62.

14. *The Interior Castle* VI, I, 164.

15. Meister Eckhart, Sermon 25, in *Meister Eckhart: Selected Writings*, 228.

16. Simone Weil, *Gravity and Grace*, 132.

SEVEN

1. Geoffrey Hill, "The Pentecost Castle, 15," in *Collected Poems* (London: André Deutsch, 1986), 144.

2. Geoffrey Hill, "The Pentecost Castle, 13," in *Collected Poems*, 143.

3. M. C. Richards, *Centering in Pottery, Poetry, and the Person*, 2nd ed. (Middletown, CT: Wesleyan University Press, 1989), 133.

4. Thomas Merton, *Monastic Journey*, ed. P. Hart (New York: Image Books, 1978), 102.

5. St. Teresa of Avila, *Interior Castle*, VI, 7, trans. M. Starr (New York: Riverhead Books, 2003), 212.

6. Meister Eckhart, *Talks of Instruction*, 9, in *Meister Eckhart: Selected Writings*, trans. and ed. O. Davies (Harmondsworth, UK: Penguin Books, 1994), 14.

7. Ibid.

8. Ibid.

9. *The Cloud of Unknowing*, chap. 32, in *The Cloud of Unknowing and other Works*, trans. A. C. Spearing (Harmondsworth, UK: Penguin Books, 2001), 55.

10. Meister Eckhart, Sermon 25, in *Meister Eckhart: Selected Writings*, 228.

11. *The Cloud of Unknowing*, chap. 13, 37.

12. Ibid.

13. *The Book of Privy Counselling*, chap. 1, in *The Cloud of Unknowing and other Works*, 104.

14. *The Cloud of Unknowing*, chap. 13, 37.

15. Ibid.

16. Ibid, 38.

17. Ibid.

18. Ibid, chap. 16, 41.

19. Ibid.

20. Meister Eckhart, *Talks of Instruction*, 12, 23.

21. Ibid., 13, 23

22. Ibid.

23. *The Cloud of Unknowing*, chap. 16, 41.

24. Patrick Kavanagh, *The Complete Poems* (Newbridge, Ireland: The Goldsmith Press, 1988), 161.

25. Julian of Norwich, *Revelations of Divine Love*, Long Text, chap. 39, trans. E. Spearing (Harmondsworth, UK: Penguin Books, 1998), 96.